GREAT

ONE LINERS

edited by Marcia Kamien

Platinum Press, LLC
2011

ISBN-13-978-1-879582-75-0

Cover by Carol Russo Design

Printed and bound in
The United States of America

98765

Having sex is like playing bridge. If you don't have a good partner, you'd better have a good hand.
-Woody Allen

Bisexuality immediately doubles your chances for a date on Saturday night.
-Rodney Dangerfield

After things have gone from bad to worse, the cycle will repeat.

Women might be able to fake an orgasm. But men can fake an entire relationship.
-Sharon Stone

My mother never saw the irony in calling me a son-of-a-bitch.
-Jack Nicholson

A fool and his money are soon partners.

To err is human, but to really foul things up requires a computer.

Do you know why they call it PMS? Because Mad Cow disease was already taken.

Great One Liners

Never do card tricks for your poker buddies.

Love is grand. Divorce is a hundred grand.

How can a two-pound box of candy make a person gain five pounds?

Before you criticize someone, you should walk a mile in their shoes. That way, when you criticize them, you're a mile away and you have their shoes.

Duct tape is like 'The Force.' It has a light side and a dark side, and it holds the universe together.

Never, under any circumstances, take a sleeping pill and a laxative on the same night.

Never mess up an apology with an excuse.

If a pig loses its voice, is it disgruntled?

Grandchildren are God's reward for not killing your kids.

We child-proofed our home three years ago ... and they're still getting in!

Oops, my brain just hit a bad sector.

See, the problem is that God gave man a brain and a penis and only enough blood to run one of them.
-Robin Williams

If a woman has to choose between catching a fly ball and saving an infant's life, she will choose to save the infant's life without even considering if there is a man on base.
-Dave Barry

Do not walk behind me, for I may not lead. Do not walk ahead of me, for I may not follow. Do not walk beside me either. Just pretty much leave me alone.

If you live in a small town, when you don't know what you're doing, someone else does.

Marriage is a 3-ring circus: engagement ring, wedding ring, suffering.

I went for a walk last night and my kids asked me how long I'd be gone. "The whole time," I told them.

Americans throw rice at weddings...do Asians throw hamburgers?

I just got skylights put into my place. The people above me are furious.

If Fed Ex and UPS merged, would they be Fed Up?

The trouble with some women is that they get all excited about nothing and then they marry him.

If a man says something in the woods and there is no woman there to hear him ... is he still wrong?

Generally speaking, you're not learning a whole lot while your mouth is moving.

ONLY IN AMERICA...

...do we buy hot dogs in packages of ten and buns in packages of eight,

...do we leave cars in the driveway and put our useless junk in the garage,

...do banks leave both doors open and then chain the pens to the counters,

...do they have drive-up ATMs with braille lettering.

The journey of a thousand miles begins with a broken fan belt and flat tire.

How come the time of day with the slowest traffic is called Rush Hour?

Be nice to your kids. They'll choose your nursing home.

Whose cruel idea was it to have the word "lisp" with an 's' in it?

Suppose you were an idiot. And suppose you were a member of Congress. But then I repeat myself.
    -Mark Twain

Government's view of the economy could be summed up in a few short phrases: If it moves, tax it. If it keeps moving, regulate it. And if it stops, subsidize it.
    -Ronald Reagan

The only difference between the tax man and the taxidermist is that the taxidermist leaves the skin.
    -Mark Twain

Keep honking. I'm reloading.

If a mute swears, does his mother wash his hands with soap?

A clean desk is the sign of a cluttered desk drawer.

Typhoon Rips Through Cemetery; 100s Dead

Police were called to a day care center because a 3-year-old was resisting a rest.

A chicken crossing the road: poultry in motion.

When the smog lifts in Los Angeles, UCLA.

A dentist and a manicurist fought tooth and nail.

Man Struck by Lightning Faces Battery Charge

I was married by a judge; I should have asked for a jury.
-Groucho Marx

What's the use of happiness? It can't buy you money.
-Henny Youngman

A boiled egg is hard to beat.

I don't feel old. I don't feel anything until noon and then it's time for my nap.
-Bob Hope

WILL ROGERS GEMS:
Never slap a man who's chewing tobacco.
Always drink upstream from the herd.
Never miss a good chance to shut up.
If you find yourself in a hole...stop digging.
There are two theories about how to argue with a woman. Neither works.
Dead batteries are given away free of charge.

When a clock is hungry it goes back 4 seconds.

Plan to be spontaneous tomorrow.

Inside every senior citizen is a younger person wondering, "What the hell happened?"

Support bacteria. They're the only culture some people have.

What happens if you get scared half to death, twice?

Okay, so what's the speed of dark?

Until I was thirteen, I thought my name was "shut up."
-Joe Namath

A will is a dead giveaway.

I went to a bookstore and asked the saleswoman where was the Self-Help Section and she said if she told me, it would defeat the purpose.
-George Carlin

The only substitute for good manners is quick reflexes.

The first testicular guard "cup" was used in hockey in 1874 and the first helmet was used in 1974.It took 100 years for men to realize that the brain is also important.

You know that indestructible black box they use on airplanes? Why don't they make the whole plane out of it?

Only in America do drugstores make the sick walk all the way to the back of the store to get their prescriptions, while healthy people can buy cigarettes at the front.

A man put an ad in the classified, Wife Wanted. Next day he got 100 letters, all saying, You can have mine.

Just think, if it weren't for marriage, men would go through life thinking they have no faults at all.

It's always darkest before dawn. So if you're going to steal your neighbor's newspaper, that's the time to do it.

Irish Coffee provides in a single glass all the major food groups: alcohol, caffeine, sugar and fat.

A clear conscience is usually the sign of a bad memory.

I wondered why the baseball kept getting bigger. Then it hit me.

A sign on the front lawn of a rehab center said, "Keep off the grass."

A dog gave birth near the road and was cited for littering.

Time may be a great healer, but it's a lousy beautician .

When I die, I want to die like my grandfather-- peacefully, in my sleep. Not screaming, like all the passengers in his car.

I think I know how Chicago got started: bunch of New Yorkers said, "Gee I'm enjoying the crime and the poverty, but it just isn't cold enough. Let's go West."
-Richard Jeni

Bigamy is having one wife or husband too many. Monogamy is the same.
-Oscar Wilde

Everybody's got to believe in something. I believe I'll have another beer.
-W.C. Fields

Never be afraid to try something new. Just remember: amateurs built the Ark; professionals built the Titanic.

My friend has kleptomania but when it gets bad, he takes something for it.

When someone says "penny for your thoughts" and you put your two-cents in, where does the extra penny go?

When cheese gets its picture taken, what does it say?

If lawyers are disbarred and clergymen defrocked, doesn't it follow that electricians can be delighted, musicians denoted, cowboys deranged, models deposed, tree surgeons debarked and dry cleaners depressed?

Why is it that if someone tells you that there are 1 billion stars in the universe you believe them, but it they tell you a wall's paint is wet, you will touch it to be sure?

It's lonely at the top, but you eat better.

The shortest distance between two points is under construction.

A verbal contract isn't worth the paper it's written on.
    -Samuel Goldwyn

Television is a medium because it is neither rare nor well done.
    -Ernie Kovaks

What grows up while growing down? A goose.

Always do sober what you said you'd do drunk. That will teach you to keep your mouth shut.
-Ernest Hemingway

You're not drunk if you can lie on the floor without holding on.
-Dean Martin

My husband and I divorced over religious differences. He thought he was God and I didn't.

Do Roman paramedics refer to I.V.s as "4's?"

Consciousness: that annoying time between naps.

The trouble with life is there's no background music.

Discretion is being able to raise your eyebrow instead of your voice.

He who dies with the most toys is still dead.

Wrinkled was not one of the things I wanted to be when I grew up.

Rap is to music as Etch-A-Sketch is to art.

The problem with the world is that everyone is a few drinks behind.
-Humphrey Bogart

Wanted: meaningful overnight relationship.

I feel sorry for people who don't drink. When they wake up in the morning, that's as good as they're going to feel all day.
-Frank Sinatra

Drunk is feeling sophisticated 'though you can't pronounce it.

The original point-and-click interface was a Smith & Wesson.

A journey of a thousand miles begins with a cash advance.

Suicidal twin kills sister by mistake!

Why do they lock gas station bathrooms? Are they afraid someone will get in and clean them?

If you try to fail and succeed at it, which have you done?

If a turtle loses its shell, is it homeless or naked?

What disease did cured ham actually have?

If a deaf person has to go to court, is it still called a hearing?

Why do people say they "slept like a baby" when babies wake up every two or three hours?

Why is an actor IN a movie, but ON tv?

How come we put a man on the moon before we realized it would be a good idea to put luggage on wheels?

The quickest way to double your money is to fold it in half and put it back in your pocket.

Time flies like an arrow. Fruit flies like a banana.

My wife and I always hold hands. If I let go, she shops.

The problem with the gene pool? No lifeguard.

I've been in love with the same woman for 49 years. If my wife ever finds out about it, she'll kill me.

There was a beautiful young woman knocking on my hotel door all night. I finally had to let her out.

Why isn't 11 pronounced "onety-one?"

Life is sexually transmitted.

The quickest way to find something lost around the house is to buy a replacement.

The best way to forget all your troubles is to wear tight shoes.

Did you hear about the old lady who talked herself out of a speeding ticket by telling the officer that she had to get there before she forgot where she was going?

I read this article that said the typical symptoms of stress are eating too much, impulse buying and driving too fast. Are they kidding? That's my idea of a perfect day!
    -Roseanne Barr

Why doesn't glue stick to the inside of the bottle?

How come just one careless match can cause a forest fire, but it takes a whole box to start a campfire?

If 4 out of 5 people suffer from diarrhea... does that mean that one of them enjoys it?

Do infants enjoy infancy as much as adults enjoy adultery?

What hair color do they put on the drivers' licenses of bald men?

Whatever happened to Preparations A through G?

You never really learn to swear until you learn to drive.

Save the whales. Collect the whole set.

The early bird may get the worm but the second mouse gets the cheese.

I drive way too fast to worry about cholesterol.

Nobody is listening until you make a mistake.

I intend to live forever. So far, so good.

For every action, there is an equal and opposite criticism.

Why did Santa's Little Helper feel bad? He had low elf esteem.

ORIGINAL BUSINESS SIGNS:
On a plumber's truck: "We repair what your husband fixed."

On a gynecologist's office: "Dr. Jones, at your cervix."

Another plumber's truck: "Don't sleep with a drip. Call your plumber."

On a tire shop: "Invite us to your next blowout."

On the Maternity Room door: "Push. Push. Push."

In a podiatrist's office: "Time wounds all heels."

In a veteranarian's office: "Back in 5 minutes. Sit. Stay."

In front of a funeral home: "Drive carefully. We'll wait."

My doctor is wonderful. Once, when I couldn't afford an operation, he touched up the X-rays.
-Joey Bishop

Great One Liners

A hangover is the wrath of grapes.

Change is inevitable except from vending machines.

Some drink at the fountain of knowledge. Others just gargle.

I haven't spoken to my wife in years. I didn't want to interrupt her.
-Rodney Dangerfield

I am a marvelous housekeeper. Every time I divorce a man, I keep the house.
-Zsa Zsa Gabor

I have an aunt who married so late in life that Medicaire picked up 80 percent of the honeymoon.

Santa Claus had the right idea: visit people only once a year.
-Victor Borge

What is a free gift? Aren't all gifts free?

I never knew real happiness until I got married. And then it was too late.

If quitters never win and winners never quit, what fool came up with "quit while you're ahead?"

Pictures of missing husbands should be put on beer cans.

Timing has an awful lot of do with the outcome of a rain dance.

Talk is cheap–except when Congress does it.

A government big enough to give you everything you want is strong enough to take everything you have.
-Thomas Jefferson

The Importance of Exercise: Exercise can add minutes to your life. This enables you, at 85 years of age, to spend an additional 5 months in a nursing home at $7,000 per month.

Where there's a will, I want to be in it.

If you are going to try cross-country skiing, start with a small country.

The only reason I would take up walking is so I could hear heavy breathing again.

Great One Liners

My grandpa started walking five miles a day when he was 60. Now he's 97 years old, and we don't know where he is.

You could run this over to your friends, but I suggest emailing it.

I have to walk early in the morning before my brain figures out what I'm doing.

We all get heavier as we get older because there's a lot more information in our heads. That's my story and I'm sticking to it.

If people from Poland are called Poles, why aren't people from Holland called Holes?

Doctor to patient: I have good news and bad news. The good news is that you are not a hypochondriac.

Can you be a closet claustrophobic?

By the time a man is old enough to watch his step, he's too old to go anywhere.

We could certainly slow the aging process if it had to work its way through Congress.

The cardiologist's diet: if it tastes good, spit it out.

Don't worry about avoiding temptation. As you get older, it will avoid you.

Did you hear about the Muslim strip club? It features full facial nudity.

Don't worry that the world ends today. It's already tomorrow in Australia.

Whoever said money can't buy happiness didn't know where to shop.

Complex problems have simple easy-to-remember wrong answers.

What is Iraq's national bird? Duck.

Help a man when he is in trouble and he will ask for your help when he is in trouble again.

The trouble with being punctual is that there's nobody there to appreciate it.
-Franklin P. Jones

Who stopped payment on my reality check?

The brain is a wonderful organ. It starts working the moment you wake up in the morning and it doesn't stop until you get into the office.
-Robert Frost

Alcohol never solves any problems, but then again, neither does milk.

You know how when people see a litter box, they say, "Oh do you have a cat?" Just once, I want to say, "No, it's for company."

Any married man should forget his mistakes; there's no use in two people remembering the same thing.

What's white and fourteen inches long?
Absolutely nothing.

If someone with multiple personalities threatens to kill himself, is it considered a hostage situation?

T-Shirt Slogans
On a child: "That's it! I'm calling Grandma!"
"My dog can lick anyone."
On a baby shirt: "Party - My Crib - 2 AM"
I'm out of estrogen and I've got a gun!
West Virginia: one million people, 15 last names

Never leave a room during a committee formation; you'll be elected.

The chances of a piece of bread falling butter side down is directly proportional to the cost of the carpeting.

Whatever hits the fan will not be evenly distributed.

You are depriving some village of its idiot.

A meeting is an event where minutes are kept and hours are wasted.

If electricity comes from electrons, does morality come from morons?

Why is air a lot like sex? It's no big deal unless you're not getting any.

Did you hear about the red ship and the blue ship that collided? Both crews were marooned.

Heck is where people go who don't believe in Gosh.

What's a witch's best school subject? Spelling.

"Doctor! Doctor! I feel like a deck of cards!"
"Sit down... I'll deal with you later."

"Doctor! Doctor! I feel like a pair of curtains!"
"Pull yourself together."

"Doctor! Doctor! I feel like a bridge!"
"What's come over you?"

Light travels faster than sound. That's why some people appear bright until you hear them speak.

Why do men want to marry virgins? Because they can't stand criticism.

How many men does it take to screw in a lightbulb? Just one. Men will screw anything.

What's the difference between a Harley and a Hoover? The position of the dirt bag.

When everything's coming your way, you're in the wrong lane, going the wrong way.

Warning: dates in calendars are much closer than they appear.

What is the best Iraqi job? Foreign Ambassador.

What's the crime committed by all transvestites? Male fraud.

What do Eskimos get from sitting too long on the ice? Polaroids.

What do you get when you cross a godfather with a lawyer? An offer you can't understand.

What do people in West Virginia do with car wrecks? Build a house next to them.

Why couldn't Dracula's wife get to sleep? Because of his coffin.

Why do ghouls and demons hang out together? Because demons are a ghoul's best friend.

When a man talks dirty to a woman, it's sexual harassment. When a woman talks dirty to a man, it's $4.99 a minute.

What's the difference between a boyfriend and a husband? 45 minutes.

What's the difference between a girlfriend and a wife? 45 pounds.

How can you tell if your wife is dead? The sex is the same but the dishes pile up.

How can you tell if your husband is dead? The sex is the same, but you get the remote.

Did you hear about the new "morning-after" pill for men? It changes your blood type.

How about the dyslexic pimp? He bought a warehouse.

What do you call 1,000 armed lesbians? Militia Etheridge.

Your gene pool could use a little chlorine.

What do anniversaries and toilets have in common? Men always miss them.

Why did Captain Kirk pee on the ceiling? He wanted to go where no man had gone before.

A man decided not to report his stolen credit card. The thief was spending a lot less than his wife did.

If all is not lost... where is it?

What does it mean when the flag at the Post Office is flying at half mast? They're hiring.

What has orange hair, big feet, and comes from a test tube? Bozo the Clone.

How about the dyslexic lawyer? He studied all year for the bra exam.

Two peanuts were walking in the park. One was a salted.

If Barbie is so popular, why do we have to buy all her friends?

Give a man a fish and he will eat for a day. Teach him how to fish and he will sit in a boat and drink beer all day.

'WHY' QUESTIONS:
Why do we nail down the lid on a coffin?
Why isn't there a special name for the tops of your feet?
Why is the third hand on a watch called the second hand?
Why is it that rain drops but snow falls?
Why is the person who invests your money called a broker?

Why isn't there mouse-flavored cat food?

If the enemy is in range ... so are you.

Isn't it strange that you never hear of a psychic winning the lottery?

Do you need a silencer to shoot a mime?

Why is it called lipstick if you can still move your lips?

If a cow laughed, would milk come out of her nose?

If you throw a cat out of the car window, is that considered kitty litter?

How did a fool and his money get together?

If corn oil comes from corn, where does baby oil come from?

If it's tourist season, why can't we shoot them?

How do they get deer to cross the road at that yellow sign?

What's another word for thesaurus?

What do they use to ship styrofoam?

What was the best thing before sliced bread?

Do hungry crows have ravenous appetites?

If a parsley farmer is sued, can they garnish his wages?

Do cemetery workers prefer the graveyard shift?

There's too much blood in my caffeine system.

If a stealth bomber crashes in the forest, will it make any sound?

Is it possible to be totally partial?

Chocolate: the other food group.

What do you do when you see an endangered animal that eats only endangered plants?

If you're cross-eyed and dyslexic, can you read okay?

Do you know how to save a drowning lawyer? No? Good.

Why did the Philharmonic have to disband? Excessive sax and violins.

Isn't it scary that doctors call what they do practice?

MORE QUESTIONS WHY:

Why do they call it a TV set, when there's only one?

Why do we drive on parkways and park in driveways?

Why are there interstate highways in Hawaii?

Why isn't phonetic spelled the way it sounds?

Why are cigarettes sold in gas stations when smoking is forbidden there?

Why is something sent by car called a shipment but something sent by ship is called cargo?

Why do they sterilize the needles for lethal injections?

If a book about failures doesn't sell, is it a success?

All generalizations are false ... even this one.

Great One Liners

If the police arrest a mime, do they tell him he has the right to remain silent?

Should vegetarians eat animal crackers?

Don't drink and drive. You might hit a bump and spill your drink.

Experience is what you get when you didn't get what you wanted.

Why do croutons come in airtight packages? Aren't they just stale bread to begin with?

How are men and parking spots alike? The good ones are already taken and what's left is handicapped.

If carrots are so good for the eyes, how come we see so many dead rabbits on the highway?

If love is blind, why is sexy lingerie so popular?

Would a fly without wings be called a walk?

How come we get just two people to choose the President of the U.S., but 50 for Miss America?

How come Tarzan doesn't have a beard?

If you read in the bathroom, is it considered multi-tasking?

Isn't Disney World a people trap run by a mouse?

We live in a strange country. If you take off all your clothes and run down the street waving a machete and firing an Uzi, terrified citizens will call the cops reporting: 'There's a naked person running around outside!'

Why do they call it Department of Interior, when it's in charge of everything outdoors?

Energizer Bunny arrested and charged with battery.

You're unique, just like everyone else.

Criminal Lawyer is a redundancy.

How do blondes' brain cells die? Alone.

Despite the cost of living, have you noticed how popular it remains?

Atheism is a non-prophet organization.

Don't take life too seriously. You won't get out alive.

Borrow money from a pessimist. They don't expect to get it back.

If you aren't educated, you'll just have to use your brain.

Don't piss me off. I'm running out of places to hide the bodies.

Artificial Intelligence usually beats real stupidity.

100,000 sperm ... and you were the fastest?

A day without sunshine is, like, night.

Boycott shampoo! Demand the real poo!

A bartender is just a pharmacist with a limited inventory.

Be more or less specific.

A conclusion is the place where you got tired of thinking.

CONFUCIOUS SAY:
.Man who stand behind car get exhausted.
.Man who stand in front of car get tired.
.Man who drive like hell bound to get there.
.Man who fight with wife all day get no piece at night.
.Virginity like bubble; one prick, all gone.

What's another word for 'synonym?'

Ever stop to think, and forget to start?

IRS: we've got what it takes to take what you got.

Prepositions are words not to ever end a sentence with.

Verbs HAS to agree with their subjects.

We have enough youth. How about a Fountain of Smart?

I used to have an open mind, but my brains kept falling out.

Forget world peace. Visualize using your turn signal.

Great One Liners

Give me ambiguity or give me something else.

How many of you believe in telekenesis? Raise my hand.

How do you know when you've run out of invisible ink?

Get a new car for your spouse; it'll be a great trade!

I just got lost in thought. It was unfamiliar territory.

Friends may come and go but enemies tend to accumulate.

I tried sniffing Coke once, but the ice cubes got stuck in my nose.

If at first you don't succeed, skydiving is not for you.

Few woman admit their age. Few men act theirs.

Wear short sleeves! Support your right to bare arms!

We were born naked, wet, and hungry. Then it got worse.

Join the Army, meet interesting people, and kill them.

Make it idiot-proof and someone will design a better idiot.

The Bermuda Triangle got tired of warm weather. It moved to Finland and now Santa Claus is missing.

If you don't mind smelling like peanut butter for two or three days, peanut butter is a darn good shaving cream.

It may be that your sole purpose in life is to serve as warning to others.

The light at the end of the tunnel is the headlamp of an oncoming train.

For every vision, there is an equal and opposite revision.

Important letters with no errors will develop errors in the mail.

Fighting for peace is like screwing for virginity.

Teamwork is essential. It allows you to blame someone else.

In front of every silver lining is a cloud.

The secret to success is sincerity. Once you can fake that, you've got it made.

I won't rise to the occasion, but I'll slide over to it.

If you can read this, I can slam on my brakes and sue you.

I took an IQ test and the results were negative.

I'm not a vegetarian because I love animals. I'm a vegetarian because I hate plants.

It IS as bad as you think and they ARE out to get you.

If voting could change things, it'd be illegal.

If you lend someone $50 and you never see that person again, it was probably worth it.

Everyone lies... but it doesn't matter, because nobody listens.

You always find something the last place you look.

Remember: in just two days, tomorrow will be yesterday.

He always wanted to be a procrastinator, but never got around to it.

There's always death and taxes. However, death doesn't keep getting worse every year.

An optimist feels that this is the best possible world. A pessimist fears this is true.

Politicians and diapers have one thing in common. They must be changed regularly and for the same reason.

Life not only begins at 40, it begins to show.

Talk is cheap because supply exceeds demand.

Brain cells come and brain cells go, but fat cells are forever.

An expert is anyone from out of town.

It's impossible for an optimist to be pleasantly surprised.

The longer you stand in line, the greater the likelihood that you're in the wrong line.

A crisis is when you can't say, "Let's just forget the whole thing."

Opportunity always knocks when you're in the shower.

When the going gets tough, everyone leaves.

Washing your car to make it rain doesn't really work.

The bigger they are, the harder they hit.

If you don't care where you are, you ain't lost.

WARNING: the consumption of alcohol may make you wonder what the hell happened to your bra and panties.

Why do psychics have to ask you your name?

When I read about the evils of drinking, I gave up reading.
-Henny Youngman

WARNING: the consumption of alcohol may cause you to think you can sing.

Without question, man's greatest invention is beer. Oh, I grant you that the wheel was also a fine invention, but the wheel doesn't go nearly as well with pizza.
-Dave Barry

WARNING: the consumption of alcohol may cause you to tell your friends over and over that you love them.

24 hours in a day. 24 beers in a case. Coincidence? I think not.

A bank is a place that will lend you money if you can prove you don't need it.

Women who seek to be equal with men lack ambition.

Shin: a device for finding furniture in the dark.

Never underestimate the power of stupid people in large groups.

Learn from your parents' mistakes. Use birth control.

Four suits for a dollar: a deck of cards.

Pride is what we have. Vanity is what others have.

A closed mouth gathers no foot.

What has 1 horn and gives milk? A milk truck.

On the other hand, you have different fingers.

Some drink at the fountain of knowledge. Others only gargle.

My mind is like a steel trap: rusty and illegal in 37 states.

The sooner you fall behind, the more time you'll have to catch up.

Love may be blind, but marriage is a real eye-opener.

Jesus loves you but everyone else thinks you're an asshole.

A diplomat is a person who can tell you to go to hell in such a way that you look forward to the trip.

Don't be irreplaceable. If you can't be replaced, you can't be promoted.

What do you call a song sung in a car? A cartoon.

What bird lifts the most? A crane.

Dolphins are so smart that within 2 weeks of captivity, they've trained people to stand at the edge of the pool and throw them fish.

Women will never be equal to men until they can walk down the street with a beer gut and a bald head, and still think they're sexy.

To steal from one person is plagarism. To steal from many is research.

Some cause happiness wherever they go... others, whenever they go.

Going to church doesn't make you a Christian any more than standing in a garage makes you an automobile.

Never hit a man with glasses. Hit him with a baseball bat.

It's not the fall that kills you; it's the sudden stop at the end.

The sole purpose of a child's middle name is so he can tell when he's really in trouble.

A bargain is something you don't need at a price you can't resist.

The enemy isn't conservatism. The enemy isn't liberalism. The enemy is bullshit.
–Lars-Erik Nelson

I'm not worried about the deficit. It's big enough to take care of itself.
-Ronald Reagan

Outside of the killings, Washington has one of the lowest crime rates in the country.
-Marion Barry, former mayor

I didn't attend the funeral, but I sent a nice letter saying I approved of it.
-Mark Twain

Whenever I feel blue, I start breathing again.

All of us could take a lesson from the weather. It pays no attention to criticism.

There are two kinds of pedestrians: the quick and the dead.

If Jimmy cracks corn and noone cares, why is there a song about him?

What do you call a pig that does karate? A pork chop.

What do you call the best butter on the farm? A goat.

I am enclosing two tickets to the first night of my new play. Bring a friend ... if you have one.
-George Bernard Shaw to Winston Churchill

Cannot possibly attend first night, will attend second ... if there is one.
-Winston Churchill, in response to Shaw

His mother should have thrown him away and kept the stork.
-Mae West

I've had a perfectly wonderful evening. But this wasn't it.
-Groucho Marx

A penny saved is a government oversight.

When the going gets tough, the tough take a coffee break.

Aim low, reach your goals, avoid disappointment.

Doing the job right gets the job done. Doing the job wrong 14 times gives you job security.

Rome did not create a great empire by having meetings. They did it by killing everyone opposing them.

Ham and eggs: a day's work for a chicken, a lifetime commitment for a pig.

I love cooking with wine. Sometimes, I even put it in the food.

What's a tree's favorite drink? Root beer.

Once over the hill, you pick up speed.

A woman has the last word in any argument. Anything a man says after that is the beginning of a new argument.

Even if you are on the right track, you'll get run over if you just sit there.

Acupuncture: a jab well done.

I'm sitting here thinking how nice it is that wrinkles don't hurt.

Give a man a fish and he'll eat for a day. Show him the internet and he won't bother you for weeks.

If ignorance is bliss, why aren't more people happy?

Some people are like Slinkies: not really good for anything; but you can't help smiling when you see them tumble down the stairs.

What has a lot of keys but cannot open any door? A piano.

You can say any foolish thing to a dog and the dog will give you a look that says, "My God, you're right! I never would've thought of that!"
  -Dave Barry

I like long walks, especially when they are taken by people who annoy me.

Marriage is a great institution, but I'm not ready for an institution yet.
  -Mae West

Every time I hear the dirty word "exercise," I wash my mouth out with chocolate.

We have 35 million laws, trying to enforce just ten commandments.

People seem to want the front of the bus; the back of the church; and the center of attention.

Today's status symbol is a cell phone clipped onto your belt. I can't afford one, so I'm wearing my garage door opener.

If you can't be kind, at least be vague.

The fortune tellers' annual dance: crystal ball.

The only time a woman wishes she were a year older, is when she's expecting a baby.

The older you are, the tougher it is to lose weight; because by then your body and your fat are really good friends.

Life is an endless struggle, full of frustrations and challenges. But eventually you will find a hair stylist you like.

Age is important only if you're cheese or wine.

Teenagers: God's punishment for having sex.

MALE OR FEMALE NOUNS

.Shoe: male, because it is usually unpolished with its tongue hanging out.

.Ziplock bags: male, because they hold everything in, but you can always see right through them.

.Hammer: male, because it hasn't evolved much over the last 5,000 years, but it's handy to have around.

.Sponges: female, because they are soft and squeezable and retain water.

.Web page: female, because it is always getting hit on.

.Kidneys: female, because they always go to the bathoom in pairs.

.Tire: male, because it goes bald and is often over-inflated.

.Hourglass: female, because over time, the weight all shifts to the bottom.

.Remote control: female, ha! You thought it would be male. But consider, it gives man pleasure, he'd be lost without it, and while he doesn't always know the right buttons to push, he keeps right on trying.

What country makes you shiver? Chile.

Why are a wise man and a wise guy opposites?

How about a fitness program for older folks called Pumping Rust?

What do bees do with honey? They cell it.

You never hear someone say, "It's only a game" when their team is winning.

The real art of conversation is not only to say the right thing at the right time, but to leave unsaid the wrong thing at the tempting moment.

If it's true that we're here to help others, then what are all the others here for?

Ever wonder what the speed of lightning would be if it didn't zigzag?

Last night I played a blank tape at full blast. The mime next door went nuts.

"I am" is reportedly the shortest sentence in the English language. Could it be that "I do" is the longest?

The only time the world beats a path to your door is when you're in the bathroom.

The trouble with being punctual is that nobody's there to appreciate it.
-Franklin P. Jones

Most people are only alive because it's illegal to shoot them.

Why is "bra" singular and "panties" plural?

Mothers of teens know why animals eat their young.

Instead of getting married again, I'm going to find a woman I don't like and just give her a house.
-Stephen Seagal

Sometimes I think war is just God's way of teaching us geography.
-Paul Rodriguez

My Mom said she learned how to swim when someone took her out on the lake and threw her off the boat. I said, "Mom, they weren't teaching you to swim."
-Paula Poundstone

If you can't be kind, at least have the decency to be vague.

One tequila, two tequila, three tequila, floor.

If it's zero degrees out today and it's supposed to be twice as cold tomorrow, how cold will it be?

Can an atheist get insurance against Acts of God?

One nice thing about egotists: they don't talk about other people.

She was only a whisky maker but he loved her still.

No matter how much you push the envelope, it'll still be stationery.

Two silkworms had a race. They ended up in a tie.

Don't join dangerous cults! Practice safe sects!

When cannibals ate a missionary, they got a taste of religion.

Honk if you love peace and quiet.

Can a hearse carrying a corpse drive in the carpool lane?

It used to be only death and taxes were inevitable. Now, there's shipping and handling.

Patient: I have a ringing in my ears. Doctor: Don't answer.

A drunk is brought in front of a judge, who tells him, "You've been brought here for drinking." The drunk says, "Okay, let's get started."

My next house will have no kitchen...just vending machines and a large trash can.

I just got back from a pleasure trip. I took my mother-in-law to the airport.

What lies at the bottom of the ocean and twitches? A nervous wreck.

How do you get holy water? You boil the Hell out of it.

Nothing is fool-proof to a talented fool.

What do you call a boomerang that doesn't work? A stick.

What do you get from a pampered cow? Spoiled milk.

What do you get when you cross a snowman with a vampire? Frostbite.

What's green and loud? A froghorn.

Great One Liners

Avoid arguments with the women in your household about leaving the seat up. Use the sink.

When a woman steals your husband, there is no better revenge than letting her keep him.

A woman is incomplete until she marries. Then she is finished.

I never knew what real happiness was until I got married and by then, it was too late.

If you want your spouse to listen...talk in your sleep.

Marriage is the triumph of imagination over intelligence.

Just think, if it weren't for marriage, men would go through life thinking they had no faults at all.

Amazing! You hang something in your closet for awhile and it shrinks two sizes!

Just as I was getting used to yesterday, along came today.

Depression is merely anger without enthusiasm.

A transvestite: a guy who likes to eat, drink, and be Mary.

What do you get when you cross a stream and a brook? Wet feet.

A husband is someone who after taking the trash out, gives the impression that he just cleaned the whole house.

I'd rather have a bottle in front of me than a frontal lobotomy.
-Tom Waits

There are three religious truths:
1. Jews do not recognize Jesus as the Messiah.
2. Protestants do not recognize the Pope as their leader.
3. Baptists do not recognize each other at the liquor store or at Hooters.

For Sale: wedding dress, size 8. Worn once by mistake.

I got a sweater for Christmas... I wanted a screamer or a moaner.

Never test the depth of water with both feet.

If you look like your passport picture, you're too ill to travel.
-Will Kommen

To attract men, I use a perfume called New Car Interior.
-Rita Rudner

Marriage certainly makes a change in passion. Suddenly you're in bed with a relative.

Everyone seems normal until you get to know them.

A 3-legged dog walks into an Old West saloon and says: "I'm lookin' for the man who shot my paw."

What's the difference between a dog and a fox? About 5 drinks.

I married Miss Right. I didn't know her first name was Always.

The most effective way to remember your wife's birthday is to forget it once.

A friend of mine confused Valium with her birth control pills. She had 14 kids but doesn't really care.

My mind not only wanders, it sometimes leaves completely.

When I bore people at a party, they think it's their fault.
-Henry Kissinger

Why is there an expiration date on sour cream?

Keep your words soft and sweet. One day, you may have to eat them.

I don't want to achieve immortality through my work. I want to achieve it through not dying.
-Woody Allen

A politician is a man who will double cross that bridge when he comes to it.
-Oscar Levant

Some mistakes are too much fun to make only once.

Never put both feet in your mouth at the same time because then you won't have a leg to stand on.

Drive carefully. It's not only cars that can be recalled by their makers.

How do we know the Indians were first in America? They had reservations.

I never drink water because of the disgusting things fish do in it.
-W.C. Fields

She's got a keen sense of rumor.

Every time I walk into a singles bar, I can hear Mom's wise words: "Don't pick that up, you don't know where it's been."

I never hated a man enough to give him back his diamonds.
-Zsa Zsa Gabor

Next Thursday there will be tryouts for the choir. They need all the help they can get.

The peacemaking meeting scheduled for today has been cancelled due to a conflict.

The only thing more important than a good education is a good parking spot at the mall.

I once wanted to become an atheist but soon gave up on the idea. They have no holidays.

"Doctor! Doctor! Help! I think I'm shrinking!"

"Calm down, please. You'll just have to be a little patient."

WASHINGTON POST PUN CONTEST WINNERS: /

Abdicate...to give up all hope of having a flat stomach.

Carcinoma...a valley in California known for heavy smog.

Lymph...to walk with a lisp.

Willy-nilly...impotent

Esplanade...to attempt an explanation while drunk.

Gargoyle...an olive-flavored mouthwash

Coffee...a person who is coughed upon.

Circumvent...the opening in the front of boxer shorts.

Balderdash...a rapidly receding hairline.

Bustard...a very rude Metrobus driver.

Testicle...a humorous question on an exam.

Flabbergasted...appalled at how much weight you've gained.

A thief broke into the local police station and stole all the bathroom equipment. The chief was quoted as saying, "Unfortunately, we have nothing to go on."

My idea of an agreeable person is a person who agrees with me.

-Benjamin Disraeli

God will pardon me. It's His business.
-Heinrich Heine

Ratio of an igloo's circumference to its diameter: Eskimo pi.

Shortest distance between 2 jokes: Straight line.

I didn't fight my way to the top of the food chain to become a vegetarian.

I take back all those times I didn't want to take a nap when I was younger.

Bad decisions make good stories.

Nothing is worse than that moment, during an argument, when you realize you're wrong.

Why aren't there directions on how to fold a fitted sheet?

I have a hard time deciphering the fine line between boredom and hunger.

LOL has gone from meaning "laugh out loud" to "I don't have anything else to say."

NEW MATH
I kilogram of falling figs=1 Fig Newton
10 cards=1 decacards
A half bath=1 demijohn
1000 grams of wet socks=1 literhosen
1000 aches=1 megahertz
Half a large intestine=1 semicolon
2200 mockingbirds=1 kilomockingbird
1 million microphones=1 megaphone
2000 lbs of Chinese soup=Won Ton
Basic unit of laryngitis=1 hoarsepower
1 millionth mouthwash=microscope

Whenever someone says, "I'm not book smart but I'm street smart," what I hear is: "I'm not really smart but I'm imaginary smart."

The only time I look forward to a red light is when I'm trying to finish a text message.

Most men would rather carry ten grocery bags in each hand than make two trips to the car.

How many times is it appropriate to say "What?" before you just nod and smile because you still didn't understand what they said.

Wicked chickens lay deviled eggs.

MapQuest really needs to start directions at #5. I'm pretty sure I know how to get out of my neighborhood.

Can't we all just agree to ignore whatever comes after DVDs? I don't want to start a whole new collection.

Isn't it strange that boxing rings are square?

While watching the Olympics I found myself cheering equally for China and the USA. No, I'm not of Chinese descent but I'm fairly certain that when Chinese athletes don't win, they're executed.

"Do not machine wash or tumble dry" means I will never wash this item, ever.

I hate leaving my house in the morning looking good and feeling confident and then not seeing anyone of importance the entire day. What a waste.

Why is a school zone 20 mph? That seems like an optimal cruising speed for a pedophile.

Even if I knew your social security number, I wouldn't know what to do with it.

Great One Liners

I keep some peoples' numbers in my phone just so I know not to answer when they call.

I used up my sick days so I'm calling in dead.

Sometimes I'll look down at my watch three consecutive times and still not know what time it is.

A flying saucer results when a nudist spills his coffee.

For people who long for peace and quiet: a phoneless cord.

Proofread carefully to see if you any words out.

There cannot be a crisis today. My schedule is already full.

How can you tell if a fax has been sent by a blonde? It has a stamp on it.

A man was asked if he talks to his wife after sex. His answer: depends if I can find a phone.

Don't feel sad, don't feel blue... Frankenstein was ugly too.

You are here: X.

The first half of our lives is ruined by our parents ... the second half, by our children.

Crime doesn't pay. Does that mean my job is a crime?

What did the bartender say to the jumper cables when they walked into the bar? Okay, you two, don't start anything.

Am I getting smart with you? How would you know?

Yes, this is my pickup. No, I will not help you move.

Sorry, I don't date outside my species.

Is it a good thing if a vacuum really sucks?

If a word is misspelled in the dictionary, how would anybody know?

If Webster wrote the first dictionary, where did he find the words?

Great One Liners

Why do we say something is out of whack? What's a whack?

Why do tug boats push their barges?

Why do we sing "Take Me Out to the Ballgame" when we're already there?

Why is it called "after dark" when it's after light?

A reporter traveling in Afghanistan was surprised to see a woman still walking 5 paces behind her husband. She was asked why, after so many other social changes, she was still doing this. The woman answered: "Land mines."

If work is so terrific, why do they have to pay you to do it?

How long a minute is depends on which side of the bathroom you happen to be.

Why do we wash bath towels? Aren't we clean when we use them?

He had delusions of adequacy.
-Walter Kerr

He has not enemies but is intensely disliked by his friends.
-Oscar Wilde

He is a self-made man and worships his creator.
-John Bright

I have never killed a man but have read many an obituary with pleasure.
-Clarence Darrow

Lady Astor to Winston Churchill: "If you were my husband I'd give you poisoned tea."
Churchill to Lady Astor: "If you were my wife, I'd drink it."

Q: Will you pass the salt?
A: How fast is it going?

I've had a perfectly wonderful evening ... but this wasn't it.
-Groucho Marx

Please, Lord, let me prove that winning the lottery won't spoil me.

Someday we'll look back on this, laugh nervously, and change the subject.

Born free ... taxed to death.

If practice makes perfect and nobody's perfect ... why practice?

A 6-year-old was asked where his grandmother lived. "Oh," he said, "she lives at the airport and when we want her we go there to get her and then when we're done having her visit, we take her back to the airport."

When in doubt, mumble.

People who live in glass houses don't have much of a sex life.

You're never too old to learn something stupid.

My shrink told me I'm crazy and I said I wanted a second opinion. Okay, he said, you're ugly, too.

Hospitality: making your guests feel like they're at home, even if you wish they were.

Knowledge is power and power corrupts. So study hard and be evil.

I think the freezer deserves a light, too.

Every day I beat my own previous record for number of days I've stayed alive.

If at first you don't succeed, find out if there's a prize for the loser.

He who smiles in a crisis has found someone to blame.

I am a nobody; nobody is perfect; therefore, I am perfect.

I don't like political jokes; I've seen too many of them get elected.

We have enough gun control; what we need is idiot control.

If God is watching us, the least we can do is be entertaining.

Better to be silent and be thought a fool, than to speak and remove all doubt.

A computer once beat me at chess but it was no match for me at kick boxing.

If sex is a pain in the ass, you're doing it wrong.

Knowledge is knowing that tomato is a fruit. Wisdom is not putting it into a fruit salad.

Evening news is when they begin with "Good evening" and then proceed to tell you why it isn't.

All the world loves a lover...except his wife.

I asked God for a bike but I know God doesn't work that way. So I stole a bike and asked God for forgiveness.

The last thing I want to do is hurt you; but it's still on the list.

The difference between in-laws and outlaws? Outlaws are wanted.

By the time a man realizes his father was right, he has a son who thinks he's wrong.

How could the cemetery raise its prices and blame it on the cost of living?

Women are like roads: the more curves, the greater the danger.

If you smoke after sex, you're doing it too fast.

Great One Liners

If Bill Gates had a penny for every time I had to reboot my computer ... oh, wait, he does!

Life's a bitch. If it was a slut, it'd be easy.

You know your kids are growing up when they stop asking where they came from and refuse to tell you where they're going.

Good health is merely the slowest way you can die.

Money talks. All mine ever says is bye-bye.

If you keep your feet firmly on the ground, you'll have a lot of trouble putting on your pants.

I used to be indecisive. Now? I'm not so sure.

I always take life with a grain of salt ... plus a slice of lemon and a shot of tequila.

Women may not hit harder but they hit lower.

TV can insult your intelligence, but nothing rubs it in like a computer.

I tried being normal once. I didn't like it.

You can catch more flies with honey than with vinegar. But who wants a bunch of flies?

A woman's place is in the home and she should go there straight from work.

A bus is a vehicle that runs twice as fast when you try to catch it than when you are sitting in it.

If you're ever tempted to fight fire with fire, remember that the Fire Department always uses water.

If winning isn't everything, why do they keep score?

Whoever coined the phrase "quiet as a mouse" has never stepped on one.

One of the quickest ways to meet new people is to pick up the wrong ball on a golf course.

If you leave me, can I come, too?

Tow truck sign: Drink and drive. We need the business.

Conserve toilet paper. Use both sides.

Booze is the answer but darned if I can remember the question.

A rabbi, a priest, and a minister walk into a bar. The bartender says, "What is this? Some kind of joke?"

A grasshopper walks into a bar and the bartender says, "You know there's a drink named after you?" The grasshopper says, "There's a drink named Kevin?"

What's round and bad-tempered? A vicious circle.

What do you do when your chair breaks? Call a chairman.

What cats like to go bowling? Alley cats.

How do dinosaurs pay their bills? with tyrannosaurus checks.

What do you call a dinosaur that smashes everything in its path? Tyrannosaurus wrecks.

What do you call a dinosaur that wears a 10-gallon hat and boots? Tyrannosaurus Tex.

What can you hold without ever touching it? A conversation.

A pizza walks into a bar and the bartender says, "We don't serve food in here."

If a tuxedo is evening wear, what is a suit of armor? Silverware.

What clothes do you get for a house? Address.

What did the boy magnet say to the girl magnet? I find you very attractive.

What did the mother broom say to the baby broom? It's time to go to sweep.

What bone will a dog never eat? A trombone.

What did the rug say to the floor? Don't move, I've got you covered.

At the end of the money, I always have some month left.

Out of estrogen. Next mood swing: two minutes.

YOU HEARD ABOUT THE DUMB BLONDE?

She called a guy to get his number.

She put lipstick on her forehead because she wanted to make up her mind.

She spent 20 minutes staring at the orange juice carton because it said, "concentrate."

She asked for a price check at the Dollar Store.

She thought a quarterback was a refund.

She tried to put M&Ms in alphabetical order.

She took a ruler to bed to see how long she slept.

She studied for a blood test.

When she heard that over 50% of all accidents happen in the home, she moved.

When she missed the 44 bus, she took the 22 bus twice.

And then there was the blonde who was taking her friend to the airport. She saw a sign that said "airport left," turned around and went back home.

What do you call a baby animal after it's six months old? Seven months old.

What do you call a guy who's born in Uruguay, moves to New York, lives in Los Angeles, and dies in Mexico? Dead.

Great One Liners

The quickest way for a parent to get a child's attention is to sit down and look comfortable.

If there's no chocolate in heaven, I'm not going.

As you get older, your secrets are safe with your friends ... they can't remember them, either.

You can't stay young forever, but you can stay immature as long as you like.

Sign outside an opera house: Barber of Seville. 200 chairs, no waiting.

How to balance the budget: tilt the country.

The doctor told me he'd have me on my feet in no time, and it worked. To pay his bill, I had to sell my car.

90% of accidents happen in the kitchen ... and my wife cooked quite a few of them.

My accountant is truly brilliant. They even named a loophole after him.

Old accountants never die; they just lose their balance.

One pigeon in a city park ate so many bread crumbs, he laid a roll.

Middle age is when it takes longer to rest than to get tired.

Gone crazy. Back soon.

The parking lot attendant had to go help out in the restaurant kitchen and in ten minutes he managed to dent six salads.

I love to go to the desert where there's nothing happening every minute.

My wife was an hour late for the honeymoon. I had to start by myself.

Why is crabgrass crabby? After all, it's winning.

I'm terrible with lawns. This year, I put in new grass and four sprinklers died.

I used to eat a lot of natural foods until I learned that most people die of natural causes.

Health nuts are going to feel stupid someday, lying in hospitals, dying of nothing.

As long as there are tests, there will be prayer in public schools.

Who was the first person to look at a cow and say, "I think I'll squeeze those dangly things and drink whatever comes out."

My take-home pay doesn't even get me home.

Forget health food. I'm at an age when I need all the preservatives I can get.

RODNEY DANGERFIELD SAID:
My wife is such a bad cook, in my house we pray after the meal
My wife's such a bad cook, the dog begs for Alka-Seltzer.
My wife is such a bad cook that when we leave dental floss in the kitchen, the roaches hang themselves.

Zen is not easy. It takes great effort to attain nothingness and then what do you have? Nothing!

Accept misfortune as a blessing. Do not wish for perfect health or a life without problems. What would you talk about?

TWISTED MEDICAL TERMS
    Tumor: one plus one more.
    Urine: opposite of you're out.
    Enema: not a friend.
    Artery: the study of paintings.
    Terminal illness: getting sick at the airport.
    Dilate: to live a long time.
    Out-patient: a person who has fainted
    Nitrates: cheaper than day rates.
    Medical staff: a doctor's cane.
    Recovery room: place to do upholstery.
    Secretion: hiding something.
    Fibula: a small lie.
    Node: I knew it.
    Caesarian Section: a neighborhood in Rome.

Why is it that when a door is open, it's ajar. But when a jar is open, it's not a door.

Men wake up as good-looking as when they went to bed; women somehow deteriorate during the night.

Make love, not war... hell, do both! Get married!

If pro is the opposite of con, then the opposite of progress is obviously Congress.

The closest I ever got to a 4.0 in college was my blood alcohol level.

A man will pay $20 for a $10 item that he needs. A woman will pay $10 for a $20 item she doesn't need but it's a bargain.

Old aunts used to come up to me at family weddings, poking me in the ribs and telling me, "You're next!" They stopped after I began doing the same thing to them at funerals.

Why do men find it difficult to make eye contact? Breasts don't have eyes.

I married my wife for her looks ... but not the ones I've been getting lately.

If life deals you lemons, make lemonade. If life deals you tomatoes, make Bloody Marys.

What do you call a musician who doesn't have a girlfriend? Homeless.

I love being married. It's great to find that one special person you want to annoy for the rest of your life.

How are women and rocks alike? You skip the flat ones.

Why is the book "Women Who Love Too Much" such a disappointment for many men? No phone numbers.

I don't do drugs any more. I can get exactly the same feeling by standing up too fast.

What do you call a handcuffed man? Trustworthy.

An Irish husband: a man who hasn't kissed his wife in twenty years, but will kill the man who does.

There's no future in time travel.

Murphy told Quinn that his wife was driving him to drink. Quinn thought he was a lucky man. His wife makes him walk.

Everyone at the funeral of the atheist felt bad. There he was, all dressed up and no place to go.

The other day, I saw a gravestone that read: "Here lies a politician and an honest man." I wonder how they got the two of them into one grave.

It takes five Irishmen to change a lightbulb: one to change it and four to remark about how grand the old bulb was.

What should you do if your husband is on the ground moaning with pain? Shoot him again.

A termite walks into a bar and says, "Is the bar tender here?"

Liquor is like love. The first kiss is magic; the second is great; the third is usual. After that, you just take off your clothes.

Radioactive cats have 18 half-lives.

A penguin walks into a bar and asks, "Has my brother been in?" "I don't know," says the bartender. "What does he look like?"

A man walks into a bar in Brooklyn and says, "What's the quickest way to Manhattan?" "Are you walking or driving?" asks the bartender. "Driving." "Well, that's the quickest way."

What's the difference between an Irish wedding and an Irish wake? One less drunk.

Two men walk into a bar. The third one ducks.

What do you call a man who knows how to control his wife? A murder suspect.

What do you get when you drive quickly through a West Virginia campus? A college degree.

Multitasking: screwing up several things at the same time.

Why don't women blink during foreplay? They don't have time.

What do you say to make 99 old ladies curse at the same time? "Bingo!"

You can't have everything. Where would you put it all?

Laughing stock: cattle with a sense of humor.

Polynesia: memory loss in parrots.

She must be older than she admits. She has a recipe for curds and whey.

You'll want a frozen bandage for cold cuts.

The way it's been going, the future tense of "invest" is "investigation."

In Dallas, a young man had himself committed to a mental institution. He was a Texan and ashamed of it!

A patient at the mental hospital said to another patient: "I'm not myself today." To which the other patient replied: "That makes four of us."

Where else but in Florida can you find people who are dreaming of a tan Christmas?

The problem with sex in the movies is that the popcorn usually spills.

Middle age is when you're faced with all kinds of temptations and you choose the one that gets you home by nine.

Middle age: when you can't turn your television off or your wife on.

I feel like I'm diagonally parked in a parallel universe.

No one is listening until you make a mistake.

Success always occurs in private but failure in full view.

Can a blind person feel blue?

Love may be blind but marriage is a real eye-opener.

Imitation is not the sincerest form of flattery. Stalking is.

Should crematoriums give discounts for burn victims?

Guns don't kill people. Postal workers do.

Some people have a way with words. Other people not have way.

I wouldn't be caught dead with a necrophiliac.

A fine is a tax for doing wrong. A tax is a fine for doing well.

I just wish the buck stopped here ... I could use a few.

Karaoke is Japanese for "tone deaf."

If you spread out all the sand in North Africa, it would cover the Sahara Desert.

Drink your coffee. There are people in India sleeping.

Help wanted: telepath. You know where to apply.

A day for firm decisions. Or is it?

3 out of 4 Americans make up 75% of the population.

A day without radiation is a day without sunshine.

A seminar on time travel will be held two weeks ago.

An unemployed court jester is nobody's fool.

Bombs don't kill people; explosions kill people.

Clairvoyants meeting cancelled due to unforeseen events.

As I said before, I never repeat myself.

Any closet is a walk-in closet if you try hard enough.

Clones are people two.

Alzheimer's advantage: new friends every day.

Cole's Law: thinly sliced cabbage.

Confucious say, Those who quote me are fools.

As long as I can remember, I've had amnesia.

An unbreakable toy is useful for breaking other toys.

Don't be a sexist. Broads hate that.

Friction can be a drag sometimes.

Help stamp out, eliminate, and abolish redundancy.

Hypochondria is the only disease I haven't got.

When I want your opinion, I'll remove the duct tape.

Have you seen Quasimodo? I have a hunch he's back!

Energizer Bunny arrested, charged with battery.

Graduates are told that the future is theirs. Then they look for jobs and find that the present is not.

A great way to make sure crime doesn't pay: let the government run it!

If they ever put a price on your head, take it!

Go away! I'd like to forget you just the way you are!

Please try to act nicely ... or don't you do imitations?

The gift that keeps on giving: a pregnant cat.

Spring is a little late this year. It must have been sent by mail.

I wouldn't touch the metric system with a 3.048 meter pole!

I've got a mind like a ... what's that thing called?

I used to be schizophrenic, but we're all right now.

A dog has a master. A cat has a staff.

If at first you don't succeed, redefine success.

Strip mining prevents forest fires.

Forgive and forget. But keep a list of names, just in case.

Hard work never killed anyone, but why take the chance?

I began with nothing and still have most of it.

Time is nature's way of keeping everything from happening all at once.

All true wisdom can be found on tee shirts.

I think sex is better than logic, but I can't prove it.

Sometimes too much to drink isn't enough.

Welcome to Utah; set your clock back 20 years.

If a thing is worth doing, it would have been done a long time ago.

A picture is worth a thousand words, but it uses up a thousand times the computer memory.

Confession is good for your soul but bad for your career.

If you think you're a person of influence, try ordering someone else's dog around.

Money isn't everything, but it sure keeps the kids in touch.

Jesus is coming, so look busy.

Losing a husband can be hard; in my case, it was almost impossible.

Seen it all, done it all, can't remember most of it at all.

When blondes have more fun, do they realize it?

My wild oats are now shredded wheat!

Two rights do not make a wrong; they make an airplane.

75.9% of all statistics are made up on the spot.

Your conscience is what hurts when all your other parts are feeling SO good.

We couldn't repair your brakes, so we made your horn louder.

If you jogged backwards, would you gain weight?

Beat the 5 o'clock rush... leave at noon!

You may be recognized soon. Hide.

I might be in the basement. I'll go upstairs and check.

I'd kill for the Nobel Peace Prize.

If I want your opinion, I'll ask you to fill out the necessary forms.

Great One Liners

If Helen Keller had ESP, would we say she had a fourth sense?

When two's company, three's the result.

Never go to sleep angry. Stay awake and plot your revenge.

The family that sticks together should bathe more often!

When I was born, they fired a 21-gun salute. Too bad they missed.

The fridge light DOES go out. Now let me out of here!!

The more you say, the less people remember.

He's dead, Jim. Kick him if you don't believe me.

If you're so smart, how come I can't understand you?

Why remember quotes when you can just make them up?

I can't remember the last time I forgot something.

Never put off 'til tomorrow what you can ignore completely.

Time is the best teacher, but it kills all its students.

Q: Should women have children over 35?
A: No, 35 kids are quite enough.

No one has ever complained of a parachute not opening.

Love is photogenic; it needs darkness to develop.

There was a man who parked his car in front of a sign that said FINE FOR PARKING.

A wife was asked what her favorite book was. "My husband's checkbook," she said.

What can you do that nobody else can?
Read my own handwriting.

What is a zebra? 26 sizes larger than an A bra.

Is it true you have a cat who can say her name?
Yes. Her name is Meow.

Man: I don't know why you wear a bra. You've got nothing to put in it.
Woman: You wear pants, don't you?

Man: How about swapping positions tonight?
Woman: Great! You stand at the sink and do the dishes while I sit on the sofa and fart.

When does a woman care for a man's company?
When he owns it.

How many honest, intelligent, caring men in the world does it take to do the dishes?
Both of them.

What do all men in singles bars have in common? They're married.

How can I increase the heart rate of my husband who is over 60?
Tell him you're pregnant.

How can I avoid getting wrinkles? Take off your glasses.

Where should an older man look for his glasses?
On his forehead.

As people age, do they sleep more soundly?
Yes, but usually in the afternoon.

How many men does it take to change a roll of toilet paper?
Who knows? It's never happened.

Why is it so difficult to find men who are sensitive, caring, and good-looking? Because they all have boyfriends.

Man says to God: "Why did you make women so attractive?" God answers: "So you'd love her."
"But God," man says, "Why make her dumb?" God says, "So she'd love you."

What is big, green, fuzzy, has four legs and would kill you if it fell from a tree? A pool table.

How do crazy people get through the woods?
They take the psycho path.

It's a good thing for her that bras can't laugh.

I'm as sound as a dollar, but I'll get better.

I know a teenager who spent a year trying to find himself. He got a haircut, and there he was!

Hash is what you get when a woman puts everything she has into her cooking.

I get tired winding up a conversation.

The four basic food groups: fresh, frozen, fast, and junk.

I knew a man who didn't have a penny to his name. So he went out and changed his name.

How do prisoners call each other? Cell phones.

"I'm sorry, but you have the wrong number."
"Are you sure?"
"Have I ever lied to you before?"

A Jew told a Christian: "We gave you the Ten Commandments."
The Christian said: "You can't say we kept them."

How do most men propose marriage? "You're going to have a WHAT?"

A famous expert on sex was giving a talk. He stood up and said, "It gives me great pleasure." And then he sat down.

I know a girl whose boyfriend doesn't smoke, drink, gamble, or chase other women. And he makes his own dresses, too!

She talks a lot because of heredity. Her mother was a woman.

Things must be very bad. The other day, the President sneaked into a café and said to the bartender, "My country doesn't understand me."

"Have you heard the latest joke about the White House?"
"I happen to work in the White House."
"That's okay, I'll tell it very slowly."

If we quit voting, will they all go away?

To all you virgins: thanks for nothing.

Fight crime. Shoot back!

Practice safe sex. Go screw yourself!

Great One Liners

Guys: no shirt, no service
Gals: no shirt, no charge

You! Out of the gene pool!

Illiterate? Write for help.

Saw it ... wanted it ... threw a fit ... got it!

Eat right. Exercise. Die anyway.

The earth is full. Go home.

I have the body of a god: Buddha.

Body by Nautilus. Brain by Mattel.

If you can't dazzle them with brilliance, riddle them with bullets.

Damned if I do, damned if I don't. So, dammit, I will!

Very funny, Scotty. Now beam down my clothes.

Sometimes I wake up grumpy. Other times, I let her sleep.

Laugh alone and the world thinks you're an idiot.

Everything you like is bad for you in some way.

A procrastinator's work is never done.

Snowmen fall from heaven, unassembled.

The most precious thing we have is life. And yet, it has absolutely no trade-in value.

Some days you're the dog, some days you're the hydrant.

Can a stupid person be a smart-ass?

Can fat people go skinny-dipping?

Man's foreplay: a half hour of begging.

If you tied buttered toast to the back of a cat and dropped it from the roof, what would happen?

All a sweater does for her is make her itch.

Why do steam irons have a permanent press setting?

Why is it that when you're driving, looking for an address, you turn down the radio?

You know how most packages say "Open here." What's the protocol if the message says, "Open somewhere else?"

If you're going at the speed of light, what happens when you turn on the headlights?

If the funeral procession is at night, do we drive with the lights off?

Where does the fire go when it goes out?

He who hesitates is not only lost, but miles from the next exit.

The only difference between a rut and a grave is the depth.

Maternity is a fact. Paternity can be a matter of opinion.

I called my acupuncturist last night and told him I was in pain. He told me to take two safety pins and call him in the morning.

BUMPER STICKERS WE HAVE SEEN:
   If you can read this, I lost my trailer.
   So you're a feminist. Isn't that cute.
   Cleverly Disguised as a Responsible Adult
   Honk if anything falls off.
   Boldly going nowhere.
   So Many Pedestrians ... So Little Time
   My other car is a Rolls Royce.

For every woman who makes a fool out of a man, there's another woman who makes a fool out of a man.

She's got a terrible inferiority complex and she's right!

I remember the good old days when it cost more to run a car than to park it.

I just bought a raffle ticket. The second prize is a car. The first prize is a parking space.

We had such a turkey for Thanksgiving dinner! He sat on my right.

A mobster is a man of convictions and he's served time on most of them.

A churchgoing Texan thinks that when he dies, he'll be allowed to stay in Texas.

We found a great way to keep visitors away. We sold the house.

Election Day: 75 million Americans take off work to vote, and about 60 of them do.

Some late-breaking election news! With six cemeteries still to be heard from, the election is too close to call.

Remember, stop lights timed for 35 mph are also timed for 70 mph.

If that phone was up your butt, maybe you could drive better.

Cover me ... I'm changing lanes.

The Earth is full. Go home!

Why does it take one million sperm to fertilize one egg? Because they won't ask for directions.

What's the mating call of a blonde?
"I'm sooooooo drunk!"

SOME BENEFITS OF BEING A WOMAN
We can be groupies. Male groupies are stalkers.
If we're dumb, someone will find it cute.
We can hug our friends without wondering if they're gay.
We can hug our friends without wondering if we're gay.
We don't look like a frog in a blender when we're dancing.
If we marry someone twenty years younger, we're fully aware we look like an idiot.

I picked up the ringing phone and said, "Who's speaking?" The answer: "You are."

"Doctor! Doctor! My hands are killing me!"
"Take them off your throat."

"Doctor! Doctor! How long have I got?"
"Ten."
"Ten what? Weeks? Months? Days?"
"10, 9, 8, 7..."

"Doctor! Doctor! A pit bull bit me on the finger."
"Which one?"
"I don't know. All pit bulls look alike to me."

How come wrong numbers are never busy?

The other day, I had a ploughman's lunch. He was not very happy about that.

What do you get when you cross LSD with a birth control pill?
A trip without the kids.

What's the definition of a gentleman? Someone who can play the bagpipes but doesn't.

Avoid the morning-after hangover. Stay drunk until noon.

I got a new rod and reel for my wife. Best trade I ever made.

If only the good die young, what does that say about our senior citizens?

If space is a vacuum, who changes the bag?

Can I play an AM radio in the evening?

How can you be alone with someone else?

Is killing time a crime?

How do you write zero in Roman numerals?

How can a person draw a blank?

Before drawing boards were invented, where did people go back to?

If tin whistles are made of tin, what are fog horns made of?

When I'm not in my right mind, my left mind gets pretty crowded.

In hospitals today, there's lot of TLC: Take Lotsa Cash!

If you don't believe there's such a thing as women's lib, try getting a back rub from a nurse's aide!

A visitor to Dallas asked the quickest way to the hospital. "Say something bad about Texas!"

They have a new device for keeping your car quiet. It fits right over her mouth.

How does the thermos know when to keep things hot and when to keep them cold?

My hometown is so small, the last one to go to bed turns out the light.

My hometown is so dull, the 7-Eleven closes at 6:00 PM.

In my hometown, the art museum is a painted turtle.

If you want something that'll last forever, take out a mortgage!

My brother-in-law borrows so much from me that, at night, my wife goes through HIS pockets.

One girl had to quit the Salvation Army. Her mother discovered she was hanging around street corners.

Somebody found out I'm an agnostic, so he burned a question mark on my lawn.

Why do Baptists object to fornication? Because it might lead to dancing!

My church welcomes all denominations: tens, twenties, fifties...

I mix religion with science. I count my blessings on a computer.

She has no social life   Even the light in her refrigerator never goes out.

Age is a very high price to pay for maturity.

They have two China's in the UN: one from column A and one from column B.

A $5 bill walks into a bar. "Get out," says the bartender. "This is a singles bar."

Six blind men walk into a bar.
"Ouch!"
"Ouch!"
"Ouch!"
"Ouch!"
"Ouch!"
"Ouch!"

How do you sink a submarine full of blondes? You knock on the door.

"Waiter, there's a dead fly in my soup."
"Yes, sir, it's the heat that kills them."

Great One Liners

"Waiter, there's a dead fly in my soup."
"It's okay, sir, no extra charge."

"Waiter, there's a dead bee in my soup."
"Yes, sir, it's the fly's day off."

"How did you find your steak, sir?"
"I moved this slice of tomato and there it was!"

"Waiter, get me a hot dog."
"With pleasure, sir."
"No, with mustard."

Did you hear about the restaurant on the moon? Great food, but no atmosphere.

The nurse who can smile when things go wrong is probably going off duty.

What's the difference between a war and a high school musical? The war causes less suffering.

What's the definition of an optimist? A folk singer with a mortgage.

"Do you love music?"
"Yes, but go ahead and play anyway."

Great One Liners

YOU KNOW YOU'RE HAVING A BAD DAY WHEN:

.Your twin forgets your birthday.

.You find your son's GI Joe dressed in drag.

.You call suicide prevention and they put you on hold.

.You turn on the evening news and they're showing emergency routes out of the city.

.The worst player on the golf course wants to play you for money.

.It costs more to fill up your car than it did to buy it.

.Your blind date turns out to be your ex-wife.

.You need one bathroom scale for each foot.

.You realize you've memorized the back of your cereal box.

.Your mother approves of the person you're dating.

.Your doctor tells you that you're allergic to chocolate chip cookies.

.Nothing you own is actually paid for.

.Your tax refund check bounces.

.Everyone loves your driver's license picture.

.You realize the phone number on the bar's bathroom wall is yours.

Man's idea of safe sex: a padded headboard.

The less we know, the longer the explanation.

What do you call cheese that isn't yours?
Nacho cheese.

What do you call Santa's helpers?
Subordinate Clauses.

What do you call four bullfighters in quicksand?
Quatro sinko.

Why do bagpipers march when they play?
They're trying to get away from the noise.

What to give to a man who has everything: a mute nymphomaniac 18-year-old girlfriend.

How do you know a woman is planning for the future? She has plastic surgery.

How do you know a man is planning for the future? He buys two cases of beer instead of one.

Husband: "Want a quickie?"
Wife: "As opposed to what?"

What do you call a blonde with half a brain?
Gifted.

Never tell your Mom her diet's not working.

Why did God create men? Because vibrators can't mow the lawn.

How many men does it take to pop corn? Three. One to hold the pan and two to show off and shake the stove.

I've been married for 37 years. Where have I gone wrong?

My wife and I went back to the hotel where we spent our honeymoon. Only this time, I stayed in the bathroom and cried.

My wife will buy anything marked down. Last month she bought an escalator.

My wife was at the beauty salon for two hours... and that was for the estimate.

My wife got a mudpack and looked great for two days. Then the mud fell off.

Thank God I'm an atheist.

Beware of the young doctor and the old barber.
-Benj. Franklin

YOU KNOW YOU'RE TRAILER TRASH WHEN...

...you have to go outside to get something from the fridge.

...the bluebook value of your truck goes up and down, depending how much gas is in it.

...you let your 12-year-old daughter smoke at the dinner table in front of her kids.

...you can't marry your sweetheart because there's a law against it.

...you lit a match in your bathroom and your house exploded right off its wheels.

...your junior prom had a day care.

...you wonder how gas stations keep their restrooms so clean.

...one of your kids was born on a pool table.

...you've been married 3 times and still have the same in-laws.

...you think a women who is "out of your league" bowls on a different night.

...you think the last words of "The Star Spangled Banner" are "Gentlemen, start your engines.

...Jack Daniels is one of your most admired people.

...you think Dom Perignon is a mafia leader.

I can give you a definite perhaps.
-Sam'l Goldwyn

If you think your boss is stupid, remember: you wouldn't have a job if he was any smarter.
-John Gotti

Don't accept your dog's admiration as conclusive evidence that you are wonderful.
-Ann Landers

A synonym is a word you use if you can't spell the other one.

The trouble with retirement is that you never get a day off.
-Abe Lemons

To you I'm an atheist; to God I'm the Loyal Opposition.
-Woody Allen

Avoid fruits and nuts; you are what you eat.
-Jim Davis

Minds are like parachutes. They work best when open.

Being young is a flaw that diminishes daily.

Drive carefully; 90% of people are accidents.

It's no accident that stressed spelled backwards is desserts.

Balanced diet: a cookie in each hand.

A diplomat is someone who thinks twice before saying nothing.

I am free of all prejudice. I hate all people equally.
-W.C. Fields

Men don't care what's on TV; they only care what ELSE is on TV.
-Jerry Seinfeld

Anyone who goes to a psychiatrist ought to have his head examined.
-Sam Goldwyn

Life is like a roll of toilet paper: hopefully long and useful, but always ending at the wrong moment.

The harder you fall, the higher you bounce.

If God wanted us to bend over, He'd put diamonds on the floor.
-Joan Rivers

Do stairs go up or down?

If the sky is the limit, then what's space? Over the limit?

Okay, says the coach, you guys line up alphabetically by height.

I take my wife everywhere, but she keeps finding her way back.
-Henny Youngman

A bird in the hand is safer than one overhead.

A word to the wise ain't necessary; it's the stupid ones who need advice.
-Bill Cosby

The making of a journalist: no ideas and the facility to express them.
-Karl Kraus

If you aren't living life on the edge, then you're taking up too much space.

Happiness is good health and a bad memory.
-Ingrid Bergman

There are two kinds of people in life: people who like their jobs and those who don't work here anymore.

Love is temporary insanity curable by marriage.

I can resist anything except temptation.

If you are willing to admit you have faults, you have one less fault to admit to.

Never insult an alligator until after you've crossed the river.

Build a man a fire and he'll be warm for a day. Set a man on fire and he'll be warm for the rest of his life.

Half of people in the world are below average.

There are 3 faithful friends: an old wife, an old dog, and ready money.

Men marry women in the hope they won't change. Women marry men in the hope they will change. Both are doomed to disappointment.

If you can't convince 'em, confuse 'em.

It is easier to fight for principles than to live up to them.

The fellow who never makes a mistake takes his orders from one who does.

There is no point in driving yourself mad trying to stop yourself going mad. You might just as well give in and save your sanity for later.
-Douglas Adams

The internet is a great way to get on the net.
-Bob Dole

I've often wanted to drown my troubles; but I can't get my wife to go swimming with me.

Technology is a way of ordering the universe so that people don't have to experience it.

What makes men chase women they have no intention of marrying? The same urge that makes dogs chase cars they have no intention of driving.

Why don't men have mid-life crises? They're stuck in adolescence.

How can you tell if a man is happy? Who cares?

What do you do with a guy who thinks he's God's Gift? Exchange him.

What's the thinnest book in the world? What Men Know About Women .

What do men and beer bottles have in common? They're both empty from the neck up.

What's the difference between men and government bonds? Bonds mature.

REAL HEADLINES FROM REAL NEWSPAPERS

Panda Mating Fails; Vet Takes Over
Miners Refuse to Work after Death
Juvenile Court to Try Shooting Defendant
Something Went Wrong in Jet Crash, Expert Says
Man Kills Self Before Shooting Wife and Son
Police Begin Campaign to Run Down Jaywalkers
War Dims Hope for Peace
If Strike Isn't Settled Quickly, It May Last Awhile
New Study of Obesity Looks for Larger Test Group
Kids Make Nutritious Snack
Local High School Dropouts Cut in Half
Cold Wave Linked to Temperatures
Couple Slain; Police Suspect Homicide

Great One Liners

Hospitals Are Used by 7 Foot Doctors
Astronaut Takes Blame for Gas in Spacecraft
Typhoon Rips Through Cemetery; Hundreds Dead
Red Tape Holds Up New Bridges
Man Struck by Lightning; Faces Battery Charges

My wife and I have the secret to making a marriage last. Twice a week, we go to a nice restaurant, have a little wine, nice food. She goes Tuesdays and I go Fridays.

I don't mind going to work. But that 8-hour wait to go home is a bitch.

When your gecko is broken, you have a reptile dysfunction.

I'd tell you to go to hell but I work there and I don't want to see you every day.

What if the Hokey Pokey really _is_ what it's all about?

Silence is golden; duct tape is silver.

Well, paint me purple and call me Barney!

After all is said and done, he never is.

Follow your dreams! Except for that one where you're naked at work.

My short-term memory isn't what it used to be. Also, my short-term memory isn't what it used to be.

I may be schizophrenic, but at least I have each other.

Kentucky: 5 million people, 15 last names.

I'm not your type; I'm not inflatable.

Reality is only an illusion that occurs due to a lack of alcohol.

Dyslexics have more nuf.

I am having an out-of-money experience.

"Do you think I'll lose my looks as I get older?" "Yes, if you're lucky."

Broken guitar for sale. No strings attached.

Behind every successful man is a woman. And behind every unsuccessful man, there are two.

ꓺENT DEFINITIONS

Avoidable: what a bullfighter tries to do.

Baloney: where some hemlines fall.

Control: a short, ugly inmate.

Detail: removing an animal's tail.

Eyedropper: a clumsy ophthalmologist.

Fire escape: way for a fire to go out.

Gossip: 24-hour teller

Hay: grass ala-mowed.

Illegal: a sick bird.

Lad: a short ladder.

Mohair: what bald men need.

Outfit: pitching a hissy-fit outdoors.

Piggyback: a lost pig comes home.

Quarterback: what you get when you pay $1 for a 75-cent item.

Reform: to gain or lose weight.

Ringworm: a worm with a bell.

Selfish: what the owner of a seafood store does.

Travelers' Aid: a soft drink for tourists.

Vitamin: what you do when someone comes to the house.

Weekend: a book with a blah ending.

Wildlife: living it up!

There should be a better way to start a day than waking up every morning.

Three weeks ago, she learned how to drive. Last week she learned how to aim it.

The wise never marry. And when they do marry, they become otherwise.

But I don't have an "ANY" key on my computer!

I can't remember the last time I forgot something.

What are three words guaranteed to humiliate men everywhere? "Hold my purse."

Right now I'm having amnesia and deja-vu at the same time. I think I forgot this before.

I bet you I could stop gambling.

Two muffins are in the toaster. One muffin says: "Man, it's hot in here!" The other muffin says: "Wow! A talking muffin!"

What's the difference between chopped beef and pea soup? Anyone can chop beef.

I can't get enough minimalism.

"Is there insanity in your family?"
"Yes, doctor, my husband thinks he's the boss."

Treat each day as if it were your last. One day you will be right.

Why did the chicken cross the road?
Don't ask me; ask the chicken.

Why did the sheep cross the road?
To get to the baa baa shop for a haircut.

Why did the fish cross the road?
It wanted to get to its school.

Why did the one-armed guy cross the road?
To get to the secondhand shop.

Why didn't the skeleton cross the road?
He had no body to go with.

Why did the rooster cross the road?
To prove he wasn't chicken.

Why did the turtle cross the road?
To get to the Shell station.

Am I ambivalent? Yes and no.

Xerox and Wurlitzer will merge to market reproductive organs.

There is no "I" in "team" but there are four in "platitude-quoting idiot."

I have friends who swear they dream in color. I say it's a pigment of their imagination.

One goldfish says to another: "If there's no God, then who keeps changing our water?"

Look out for #1 ... and don't step in #2, either.

A fool and his money can throw one hell of a party.

Department of Redundancy Department

This is your cell phone company. We just found out you're too dumb to use your phone, so please place it on the ground and start jumping on it. Thank you.

I've been on so many blind dates, I should get a free dog.

Sacred cows make the best hamburgers.

Do not follow, for I may not lead. Do not lead, for I may not follow. Just go over there somewhere, please and be quiet.

Contents may have settled out of court.

Letting the cat out of the bag is a whole lot easier than trying to get it back in.

I'm one bad relationship away from having thirty cats.

I think it's about time I told you what people say behind your back: nice ass.

How do you keep an idiot amused? Keep watching this message until it goes away.

Why do bankruptcy lawyers expect to be paid?

Chastity is curable if detected early enough.

Smokers are just like everyone else ... just not as long.

She's always late. Her ancestors arrived on the Juneflower.

Back up my hard drive? How do I put it in reverse?

This isn't an office. It's Hell with fluorescent lighting.

Not all men are annoying. Some are dead.

Stress is when you wake up screaming and you realize you haven't fallen asleep yet.

Suburbia: where they tear out the trees and then name streets after them.

See no evil, hear no evil, date no evil.

Remember, the Bible was written by the same people who believed the earth was flat.

If I throw a stick, will you leave?

A woman's favorite position is CEO.

If I want to hear the pitter patter of little feet, I'll put shoes on my cats.

I'm trying to imagine you with a personality.

Life: too many freaks, not enough circuses.

I have a computer, a vibrator, and pizza delivery. Why should I leave the house?

I'd like to have more self-esteem, but I don't deserve it.

Two wrongs do not make a right, but three lefts do.

I like kids, but I don't think I could eat a whole one.

Chaos, panic, and disorder... my work here is done.

Macho Law prohibits men from admitting they're wrong.

I plead contemporary insanity.

Sadly, since I went on the wagon, the wagon went and got a liquor license.

When a girl says, "No," she really means "Yes;" but not with you.

Sure you can't take it with you. But you can hide it where nobody else will ever find it.

My wife says my sex drive has taken up walking.

We had a great neighborhood watch going when I was kid. And then she closed her drapes.

False hope is nicer than no hope at all.

A good scapegoat is nearly as good as a solution to the problem.

I don't know what your problem is, but I'll bet it's pretty hard to pronounce.

You sound reasonable. Time to up my meds.

It might look like I'm doing nothing; but at the cellular level, I'm actually quite busy.

I'm glad I'm not as judgmental as all those self-righteous, censorious, stupid people here.

Today I will gladly share my experience and advice, for there are no sweeter words than "I told you so."

Death to all fanatics!

You no longer need to punish, deceive, or compromise yourself. Unless, of course, you want to stay employed.

What am I? Flypaper for freaks?

I assume full responsibility for my actions–except the ones that are someone else's fault.

Do they ever shut up on your planet?

The fact that no one understands you doesn't mean you're an artist.

Any connection between your reality and mine is purely coincidental.

Your birth certificate is an apology letter from the condom factory.

Don't bother me. I'm living happily ever after.

You say I'm a bitch like it's a bad thing!

Whisper my favorite words in my ear: "I'll buy it for you."

Therapy is expensive. Popping bubble wrap i cheap. Your choice.

Sarcasm is just one more service I offer.

I'll try to be nicer if you'll try to be smarter.

I like you. You remind me of when I was young and stupid.

I'm out of my mind, but feel free to leave a message.

I have plenty of talent and vision. I just don't give a damn.

How about never? Is never good for you?

Don't worry, I forgot your name too.

Drink 'til she's cute, but stop before the wedding.

I'm not cheap but I am on special this week.

He who hesitates is boss.

It's a small world but I wouldn't want to paint it.

If you can't read this, you're illiterate.

It's wrong to ever split an infinitive.

And don't start a sentence with a conjunction.

Also, too, never, ever use repetitive redundancies.

In elementary school, in case of fire you're supposed to line up quietly in single file, from smallest to tallest. What is the logic? Do tall people burn slower?

What's Wal-Mart? Do they, like, make walls there?
-Paris Hilton

Death is life's way of saying, "You're fired!"

YO MAMA JOKES
Yo Mama is so bald, I can read her mind!
Yo Mama is so fat, she has her own gravitational pull.
Yo Mama is so fat, she needs 2 watches, one for each time zone.
Yo Mama is so fat that when she gets on the scale it says "to be continued."

Yo Mama is so fat, she could sell shade.

Yo Mama is so fat, I had to take a train and two buses, just to get on her good side.

Yo Mama is so fat, when she crosses the street, cars look out for her.

Yo Mama is so stupid, she tripped over a cordless phone.

Yo Mama is so old, her SS# is 000-00-0001!

Yo Mama is so poor, she couldn't afford to scratch an itch.

Yo Mama is so dumb, she flunked recess!

Yo Mama's so stupid, she tried to drown a fish.

Yo Mama is so dumb, she brought a spoon to the Super Bowl.

Yo Mama's so poor, she can't pay attention.

I don't work here. I'm a consultant.

"Whenever I watch TV and see those poor starving kids all over the world, I can't help but cry. I mean, I'd love to be skinny like that but not with all those flies and death stuff."

-Mariah Carey

"If you ever see me getting beaten by the police, put down the video camera and come help me."

-Bobcat Goldthwait

I can see your point, but I still think you're full of crap.

Black holes are where God divided by zero.

Never play strip poker with a nudist; they have nothing to lose.

When the chips are down, the buffalo's empty.

Lawyer's creed: a man is innocent until proven broke.

AMAZING TRUE FACTS

The metal backs of iPods are made from recycled zippers.

Every sixteen minutes, somebody named Richard dies.

The original title for Catcher in the Rye was Hey, Look! A Carousel!

Eskimos don't believe in bridges or tunnels.

Dolphins kill more people annually than sharks and influenza combined.

Billy Bob Thornton's grandfather was the first person to own a television.

On a dare, former President Rutherford B. Hayes declared war on Chile, for 17 minutes.

Great One Liners

What does a blonde think an innuendo is? An Italian suppository.

How did the blonde try to kill a bird? She threw it off the cliff.

What did the blonde say when she saw the YMCA sign? "Look, they spelled Macy's wrong."

It was so cold last winter, I saw a lawyer with his hands in his own pockets.

I really think the Mars Rover is scouting for the next Wal-Mart site.

Why don't Jewish mothers drink? It interferes with their suffering.

Most Texans think Hanukkah is some kind of duck call.
-Richard Lewis

A Jewish telegram: "Start worrying. Details to follow."

I can see clearly now, the brain is gone.

Dain Bramaged

Television is a medium because it's neither rare nor well done.
-Ernie Kovaks

If at first you <u>do</u> succeed, try not to look astonished.

2 + 2 = 5 for extremely large values of 2.

Do witches run spell checkers?

Honk if you love peace and quiet.

It's not hard to meet expenses. They're everywhere.

I have enough money to last me the rest of my life. Unless I buy something.
-Jackie Mason

Everybody likes a kidder, but nobody loans him money.
-Arthur Miller

Whoever called it necking was a poor judge of anatomy.
-Groucho Marx

With the collapse of vaudeville, new talent has no place to stink.
-George Burns

I went on a diet, quit heavy drinking, and in 14 days I had lost exactly two weeks.
-Joe E. Lewis

The things that come to those who wait may very well be the things left behind by those who got there first.

Bankruptcy is a legal proceeding in which you put your money in your pants pocket and give your coat to your creditors.
-Sam Goldwyn

The remarkable thing about my mother is that for 30 years, she served nothing but leftovers. The original meal has never been found.
-Calvin Trillin

If you lined up all the cars in the world, end to end, someone would still try to pass them.

Those who live by the sword get shot by those who don't.

COMPUTER TALK

Access denied. Nyah, nyah, nyah

As a computer, I find your faith in technology amusing.

100% file compression: DELETE

Senile.com found. Out of memory.

An upgrade: take out all the bugs and put new ones in.

File not found. Fake it? (Y/N)

Breakfast.com halted. Cereal port not responding.

A computer's attention span is as long as its power cord.

Computer: a device designed to speed and automate errors.

Remember, if the world didn't suck, we'd all fall off.

Latest surveys show that 3 out of 4 people make up 75% of the world's population.

How do you keep your husband from reading your email?

Rename the mail folder "Instruction Manuals."

Waiter, do you have frog's legs?
No, sir, I've always walked like this.

Waiter, this egg is spoiled.
Don't blame me, sir, I only laid the table.

Waiter, this coffee is awful. It tastes like dirt.
Yes, sir, it was ground yesterday.

Experience: a comb that life gives you after you've gone bald.

What do you call that useless piece of skin on the end of a man's penis?
His body.

What does it mean when a man is in your bed gasping for breath and calling your name?
You didn't hold the pillow down long enough.

Why do men give names to their penises?
They don't like the idea of having a stranger make 90% of their decisions.

How many men does it take to screw in a light bulb?
One. He holds it there and waits for the world to revolve around him.

What do men and pantyhose have in common?

They either cling, run, or don't fit right in the crotch.

There is always free cheese in a mousetrap.

OLD IS WHEN...

...your sweetie says, "Let's go upstairs and make love," and you say, "Honey, I can't do both."

...your friends like your new alligator shoes and you're barefoot.

...you are cautioned to slow down by the doctor, not the police.

..."getting a little action" means you don't need any extra fiber today.

..."getting lucky" means finding your car in the parking lot.

...an "all-nighter" means not getting up to pee.

...a sexy babe catches your eyes and your pacemaker opens the nearest garage door.

You may have a heart of gold ... but so does a hard-boiled egg.

The only thing you get without trying is dandruff.

Statistics are like bikinis. What they reveal is suggestive, what they hide is essential.

Inflation is when the buck doesn't stop anywhere.

Bachelor: a man who is footloose and fiancee free.

You show me a child who's not playing with toys and I'll show you a father who's not finished with them yet.

Ballerinas are always on their toes. Why don't they just hire taller ballerinas?

Regular naps prevent old age–especially if you take them while driving.

Talk is cheap except when Congress does it.

Marriage is a relationship where one person is always right and the other one is the husband.

Laziness is nothing more than the habit of resting before you are tired.

Those who can't laugh at themselves leave the job to others.

I love oral sex ... it's the phone bill I hate.

You can't buy love, but you pay heavily for it.

A child's greatest period of growth is a month after you've purchased new school clothes.

Bad officials are elected by good citizens who do not vote.

Saving is such a good idea. Especially when your parents have done it for you.

Someday we'll look back on all this and plow into a parked car.

There is only one perfect spouse in the world; and the neighbor has it.

Wife: darling, today is our anniversary... what should we do?
Husband: let's stand in silence for 2 minutes.

90% of men kiss their wife goodbye when they leave their house. The rest kiss their house goodbye when they leave their wife.

A young person knows the rules but an older person knows the exceptions.

A million deaths is a statistic; a single death is a tragedy.

The secret to success is knowing who to blame for your failures.

A man walked into the doctor's office, and said, "Doctor, I've hurt my arm in several places."
Said the doctor: "Well, don't go there any more."

I almost had a psychic girlfriend, but she left me before we met.

If everything seems to be going well, you have obviously overlooked something.

Did you ever walk into a room and forget why you were there? I think that's how dogs spend their lives.
-Sue Murphy

I have six locks on my door, all in a row. When I go out, I lock every other one. I figure, no matter how long someone stands there picking the locks, they're always locking three.
-Elaine Boosler

Never trust a dog to watch your food.

Great One Liners

I was a vegetarian until I started leaning toward sunlight.
-Rita Rudner

The statistics on sanity are that one of every four Americans is suffering from a mental illness. Think of your three best friends. If they're okay, then it's you.
-Rita Mae Brown

When you look at Prince Charles, don't you think that someone in the Royal Family knew someone in the Royal Family?
-Robin Williams

How come when we talk to God, we're praying; but if God talks to us, we're schizophrenic?
-Lily Tomlin

Why does Sea World have a seafood restaurant? I'm halfway through my fishburger when I suddenly think, What if I'm eating a slow learner?
-Lynda Montgomery

Our bombs are smarter than the average high school student. At least they can find Kuwait.
-A. Whitney Brown

Lady: Sir, you are drunk.

W. Churchill: And you are ugly. The difference is that tomorrow I will wake up sober.

LITTLE JOHNNY

The teacher sends Little Johnny to the map to find North America. He finds it.

Teacher: Very good. Now, class, who discovered North America?

Class: Little Johnny!

Teacher: Little Johnny, give me a sentence beginning with "I."

Little Johnny: "I" is...

Teacher: No, no. Always say "I am."

Little Johnny: "Okay. I am the ninth letter of the alphabet.

Teacher: What is the chemical formula for water?

Little Johnny: H, I, J, K, L, M, N, O

Teacher: What are you talking about?

Little Johnny: Well, yesterday you told us the chemical formula for water is H 2 O.

Teacher: What's someone called who keeps talking after nobody's interested?

Little Johnny: A teacher!

Teacher: Can anyone give an example of "coincidence."

Little Johnny: My mother and my father got married on the same day.

Teacher: What a strange pair of socks you have on today, Little Johnny. One is green and one is red with orange dots.

Little Johnny: It is strange. I have another pair like this at home.

Teacher: Do you say prayers before meals?

Little Johnny: No, ma'am, I don't have to. My mother is a good cook.

Teacher: Your composition on "My Dog" is exactly the same as your brother's. Did you copy?

Little Johnny: Oh, no. It's the same dog.

Teacher: How do you spell crocodile?

Little Johnny: K-R-O-K-A-D-I-L

Teacher: That's totally wrong!

Little Johnny: You asked how I spell it.

He was a man of great statue.
-Thos. Menino, Boston mayor

Say NO to negativity.

Republicans understand the bondage between mother and child.
-Dan Quayle

We cannot let terrorists and rogue nations hold this nation hostile or our allies hostile.
-George W. Bush

You can't believe everything you hear, but you can repeat it.

This is unparalyzed in the state's history.
-Gib Lewis, Texas Speaker of the House

The police are not here to create disorder, they're here to preserve disorder.
-Richard Daley, former Chicago mayor

He's going up and down like a metronome.
-Ron Pickering

I just might fade into Bolivian, you know what I mean?
-Mike Tyson, boxer

Marie Scott ... has really plummeted to the top.
-Alan Weeks

Well, that was really a cliff-dweller.
-Wes Westrum, about a close ball game

It's beyond my apprehension.
-Danny Ozark, baseball team manager

You could've knocked me over with a fender.
-Jane Ace

The doctors x-rayed my head and found nothing.
-Dizzy Dean

I owe a lot to my parents, especially my mother and father.
-Greg Norman

The streets are safe in Philadelphia; it's only the people that make them unsafe.
-Frank Rizzo, former mayor & police chief

Q: If you could live forever, would you and why?
Miss Alabama 1994: I would not live forever because we should not live forever, because if we were supposed to live forever, then we <u>would</u> live forever, but we cannot live forever which is why I would not live forever.

A will is a dead giveaway.

God did not create the world in seven days; he messed around for six days and then pulled an all-nighter.

I haven't committed a crime. What I did was fail to comply with the law.
-David Dinkins, NYCity mayor

CONFUCIUS SAY
Man who behaves like an ass will be butt of many jokes.

Foolish man give wife grand piano. Wise man give wife upright organ.

Man who think he is number one must remember that this number is next to nothing.

Man who stands on toilet is high on pot.

Man who makes love in grass gets piece on earth.

Wash face in the morning, neck at night.

Bird in hand makes hard to blow nose.

Man who cuts self while shaving loses face.

Great One Liners

Man who eats photo of father soon spitting image of father.

Man who crosses ocean twice without washing hands is dirty double crosser.

Man who tell one too many light bulb jokes soon burn out.

Woman who wear jock strap have make-believe ballroom.

Man who pushes piano down mineshaft gets tone of A flat miner.

Woman who put man in doghouse soon find him in cathouse.

Man who fight with wife all day get no piece at night.

Man who sit on tack gets point.

Confucius say too damn much.

The buck doesn't even slow down here.

Inflation is when the buck doesn't stop anywhere.

If you can read this, roll me over.

Instead of trying to read this bumper sticker, maybe you should watch the road?

Hey, baby, you've got something on your butt... my eyes.

An archeologist is someone whose life is in ruins.

I believe we should all pay our taxes with a smile. I tried—but they wanted cash.

Having a child makes you a parent; with two, you become a referee.

THE THINGS PEOPLE REALLY SAY!
.My sister has extra-century perception.

.It's the people I tell things to that can't keep a secret, it's not me.

.I guess I'll have to start from scraps.

.Good punctuation means not to be late.

.He had to use a fire distinguisher.

.I can't eat on an empty stomach.

.He's a wolf in cheap clothing.

.I'm scared to death to get sick.

.If people don't want to come to the ballpark, nobody can stop them.

If bills are rectangular, how come they keep rolling in?

If evolution really works, how come mothers have only two hands?

My friend Sophie is so proud. Her son sees a psychiatrist and they spend a whole hour talking about her.

What shall we do, sir? The enemy are as thick as peas!
Shell them, of course!

Parrots prefer short words. No Polly-syllables.

Sex is overrated. But can you imagine where everything else stands?

They now have a teenager doll. You wind it up and it resents you for it.

Think of it this way. Your phone is another man's wrong number.

How to drive someone crazy: send an email message saying "Disregard previous message."

He's really laid back. It takes him two hours to watch "60 Minutes."

Never put off until tomorrow what you can put off until the day after tomorrow.

I know a topless lady ventriloquist. Nobody has ever seen her lips move.

I lived in a tough neighborhood. If you weren't home by midnight, you were declared dead.

Last year, we took a trip around the world. This year, we're going somewhere else.

A twin came home from a late date and told her sister, "We're not identical any more."

Gossips are the spies of life.

A virgin is a woman who thinks all men are created equal.

CLASSIC WOODY ALLEN
When we played softball, I'd steal second base, feel guilty, and go back.

I can't listen to that much Wagner. I start getting the urge to conquer Poland.

My luck is getting worse and worse. Last night, for instance, I was mugged by a Quaker.

I was thrown out of NYU. On my metaphysics final, they caught me cheating. I looked within the soul of the boy sitting next to me.

In California, they don't throw their garbage away. They make it into TV shows.

Some guy hit my fender, and I told him, "Be fruitful and multiply," but not in those words.

CLASSIC GEORGE CARLIN
A house is just a place to keep your stuff while you go out and get more stuff.

What year did Jesus think it was?

The reason I talk to myself is because I'm the only one whose answers I accept.

Weather forecast for tonight: dark. Continued dark overnight, with widely scattered light by morning.

Religion has convinced people that there's an invisible man...living in the sky. Who watches everything you do every minute of every day. And the invisible man has a list of ten specific things he doesn't want you to do. And if you do any of these things, he will send you to a special place, of burning and fire and smoke and torture and anguish for you to live forever, and suffer and burn and scream, until the end of time. But he loves you. He loves you. He loves you and he needs money.

If the Cincinnati Reds were really the first major league ball team, who did they play?

Have you ever noticed that their stuff is shit but your shit is stuff?

As soon as someone is identified as an unsung hero, he no longer is.

The IQ and life expectancy of Americans recently passed each other in opposite directions.

If it is true that our species is alone in the universe, then I'd have to say that the universe aimed rather low and settled for very little.

Ever notice that anyone going slower than you is an idiot, but anyone going faster is a maniac?

In America, anyone can become President. That's the problem.

Do you think Sammy Davis ate Junior Mints?

RITA RUDNER CLASSICS

In Hollywood, a marriage is successful if it outlasts milk.

I wonder if other dogs think poodles are members of a weird religious cult?

We've begun to long for the pitter-patter of little feet, so we bought a dog. Well, it's cheaper and you get more feet.

Men who have a pierced ear are better prepared for marriage. They've experienced pain and bought jewelry.

My boyfriend and I broke up. He wanted to get married and I didn't want him to.

The word aerobics came about when gym instructors said, If we're going to charge so much, we can't call it jumping up and down.

Some cars have things that last a lifetime: payments!

My wife makes the budget work. We go without a lot of things I don't really need.

What's the best way to prevent infection from biting insects?
Don't bite any.

In Jersey, the mosquitoes show up on radar.

A bird in the hand is terrible table manners.

I have to spend a lot of money on food. My family won't eat anything else.

We claim this country was founded in 1776. The Indians want to know when it was losted.

How does a nude show have a dress rehearsal?

The cops raided a live sex show. They gave it one year to get out of town.

'I was out with a nurse last night."
"Well, maybe if you behave, they'll let you out without one."

Two can live as cheaply as one can play golf.

I have a friend who needs psychological help. He thinks golf is a game.

A Scotsman gave up the game of golf after 20 years. He lost his ball!

I met my wife at a dance. It was so embarrassing! I thought she was home with the kids.

We've been happily married for ten years. Ten out of thirty ain't bad!

In my old neighborhood, the most common form of transportation was a stretcher.

Nothing needs changing more than your neighbor's habits.

MORE CLASSIC WOODY ALLEN

Basically, my wife was immature. I'd be at home in the bath and she'd come in and sink my boats.

I am thankful for laughter, except when milk comes out of my nose.

I will not eat oysters. I want my food dead. Not sick, not wounded ... dead.

I'm short enough and ugly enough to succeed all on my own.

I failed to make the chess team because of my height.

How am I immature? Intellectually, emotionally, and sexually. Yeah, but in what other ways?

I'm so excited...I think today I'll brush all of my teeth.

Organized crime in America takes in over 40 billion dollars a year and spends very little on office supplies.

When I was kidnapped, my parents snapped into action. They rented out my room.

My education was dismal. I went to a series of schools for mentally disturbed teachers.

Students achieving Oneness will move on to Twoness.

I'm astounded by people who want to know the universe when it's hard enough to find your way around Chinatown.

I tended to place my wife under a pedestal.

I took a speed reading course and read War and Peace in twenty minutes. It involves Russia.

I have bad reflexes. I was once run over by a car being pushed by two guys.

MORE CLASSIC GEORGE CARLIN

Swimming is not a sport. Swimming is a way to keep from drowning.

Honesty may be the best policy but it's important to remember that apparently by elimination dishonest is the second-best policy.

People ask, "Can I ask you a question?" Didn't give me much of a choice there, did you, buddy?

Beethoven was so hard of hearing he thought he was a painter.

George Washington's brother, Lawrence, was the Uncle of Our Country.

Bowling is not a sport because you have to rent the shoes.

I'm always relieved when someone is giving a eulogy and I realize I'm listening to it.

CLASSIC ROSEANNE BARR

When my husband comes home, if the kids are still alive, I figure I've done my job.

My husband said he needed more space. So I locked him outside.

Experts say you should never hit your children in anger. When is a good time? When you're feeling festive?

It's okay to be fat. So you're fat. Just be fat and shut up about it.

I'm not going to vacuum 'til Sears makes one you can ride on.

Great One Liners

In Tulsa, restaurants have signs that say Sorry, we're open.

My wife wanted to see my paycheck go further, so she took it to Paris.

Middle age is when it takes longer to rest than to get tired.

Patriotism, for some, is the willingness to make any sacrifice, as long as it doesn't hurt business.

It was raining so hard, I got seasick walking home.

I just finished my first book. Next week I may read another one.

Keep your eyes glued to this book. That way, you'll know where they are.

My wife knows how to make a long story short. She interrupts.

I bought my wife a mink. She keeps the cage so clean!

To write with a broken pencil is pointless.

"Children, what comes after O?"
"Yeah!"

A backward poet writes inverse.

A grenade fell onto a kitchen floor in France, resulting in linoleum blown apart.

He broke into song because he couldn't find the key.

The math professor went crazy with the blackboard. He did a number on it.

With her marriage, she got a new name and a dress.

THE FOUR STAGES OF LIFE:
    1) You believe in Santa Claus.
    2) You don't believe in Santa Claus.
    3) You are Santa Claus.
    4) You look like Santa Claus.

A calendar's days are numbered.

You are stuck with your debt if you cannot budge it.

GREAT TRUTHS LITTLE KIDS HAVE LEARNED

1) No matter how hard you try, you cannot baptize cats.

2) When your Mom is mad at you, don't let her brush your hair.

3)If your sister hits you, don't hit her back. They always catch the second person.

4) Never ask your 4-year-old brother to hold a tomato.

5) Don't sneeze when someone is cutting your hair.

6) Never hold a Dust-Buster and a cat at the same time.

7) You can't hide a piece of broccoli in a glass of milk.

8) Don't wear polka dot underwear under white shorts.

Men can read maps better than women. 'Cause only the male mind could conceive of one inch equalling 100 miles.

-Roseanne Barr

What is the difference between a man and a catfish? One is a bottom-feeding scum sucker; and the other is a fish.

DIFFERENT DEFINITIONS
    Arcade: a drink served on Noah's Ark.
    Band-Aid: a fund to help a rock band.
    Cadillac: shortage of cattle.
    Cowlick: bashing a cow.
    Doughnut: holey food
    Eclipse: what a Cockney barber does for a living.
    First Lady: Eve
    Fire Escape: a way for the fire to go out.
    Goodbye: a bargain.
    Hatchet: what a hen does to an egg.
    Installment: putting a horse in his stall.
    Life Jacket: a special coat that lasts a lifetime.
    Moth Ball: a special social event for moths.
    Network: the process of making nets.
    Oyster bed: a place for an oyster to sleep.
    Pigment: a mint plant grown to feed hogs.
    Relief: what trees do in Spring.
    Showoff: the show has been cancelled.
    Time keeper: the guy who didn't return your watch.
    Well done: a water, gas, or oil well is finished.
    Writer: one who corrects a wrong.

What does a man consider a seven-course meal? A hot dog and a six-pack of beer.

I think, therefore I am. I think.

GREAT TRUTHS THAT ADULTS HAVE LEARNED
1) Raising teenagers is like nailing jelly to a tree.
2) Wrinkles don't hurt.
3) Families are like fudge: mostly sweet, with a few nuts.
4) Today's mighty oak is yesterday's acorn that held its ground.
5) Laughing is good exercise, like laughing on the inside.
6) Middle age is when you choose your cereal for the fiber, not the toy.

Saleswomen hold up an ugly dress and say, "It looks much better on." On what? On fire?

Waiter, there's a fly in my soup!
Keep it down, sir, or they'll all be wanting one.

SUCCESS
.At age 4, success if not peeing in your pants.
.At age 12, success is having friends.
.At age 17, success is having a driver's license.
.At age 35, success is having money.
.At age 50, success if having money.
.At age 70, success if having a driver's license.
.At age 75, success if having friends.
.At age 80, success is not peeing in your pants.

Growing old is mandatory; growing up is optional.

You're getting old when you get the same sensation from a rocking chair that you once got from a roller coaster.

CLEVER ANAGRAMS
An anagram is one word or phrase, with the letters rearranged to make another word or phrase.

DORMITORY
DIRTY ROOM

PRESBYTERIAN
BEST IN PRAYER

THE MORSE CODE
HERE COME DOTS

ANIMOSITY
IS NO AMITY

ELECTION RESULTS
LIES - LET'S RECOUNT

SLOT MACHINES
CASH LOST IN ME

Great One Liners

DESPERATION
A ROPE ENDS IT

THE EYES
THEY SEE

ASTRONOMER
MOON SHARER

SNOOZE ALARMS
ALAS! NO MORE Z'S

ELEVEN PLUS TWO
TWELVE PLUS ONE

A DECIMAL POINT
I'M A DOT IN PLACE

MOTHER-IN-LAW
WOMAN HITLER

GEORGE BUSH
HE BUGS GORE

I told my girlfriend I got a job in a bowling alley. She said, "Ten Pin?" I said, "No, permanent."

Marriage is the chief cause of divorce.

Great One Liners

If you live to be 100, you've got it made. Very few people die after that age.
-George Burns

I was reading this book today, "The History of Glue." I couldn't put it down.

I visited the offices of the ASPCA today. It's tiny; you couldn't swing a cat in there.

Waiter, there's a fly in my soup!
Oh, no, that one? He comes here every night.

I went into a pet shop and asked to buy a goldfish. "Do you want an aquarium?" asked the clerk. I said, "I don't care what star sign it is."

I went to buy a watch and the man said, "Analog?" I said, "No, just a watch."

I told the doctor that I'm scared of lapels. "You have cholera," he said.

I met the man who invented crosswords. I can't remember his name ... P blank T blank R.

I bought some Armageddon cheese in the supermarket today. It said "Sell before End."

I went to see a job counselor. He said, "How about volunteer work?" I said, "I wouldn't do that if they paid me."

A cowboy walks into a German car showroom and says, "Audi!"

You know the honeymoon is pretty much over when you start to go out with the boys on Tuesday nights–and so does she.

Marriage is the triumph of imagination over intelligence. Second marriage is the triumph of hope over experience.

Men are all the same. They just have different faces so you can tell them apart.

Eighty percent of married men cheat in America; the rest cheat in Europe.

A good pun is its own reword.

Like most people my age, I'm 30.

If you want to find a committed man, look in a mental hospital.

Is it fair to say there would be less litter if blind people were given pointed canes?

I haven't slept for 10 days, because that would be too long.

If I understood Morse Code, I imagine going to see tap dancing would drive me nuts.

An invisible man married an invisible woman. Their kids were nothing to look at, either.

I discovered I was dyslexic when I went to a toga party dressed as a goat.

What did the magic tractor do? It turned into a field.

In this age of recession, Bob the Builder has changed his name. To Bob.

I started writing poetry the other day.
P O E T R   That's coming along nicely.

How many Alzheimer's patients does it take to change a lightbulb?
To get to the other side.

Did you hear about the dyslexic devil-worshipper? He spent his life worshipping Stan.

Take my advice. I don't use it anyway.

How do you feel about women's rights? I like both sides of them.

In my family tree, my gay cousin is in the fruit section.

When I was a kid, my parents moved a lot; but I always found them.

Military intelligence is a contradiction in terms.

Either this man is dead or my watch has stopped.

I don't have a drinking problem except when I can't get a drink.
-Tom Waits

I told my wife I was seeing a psychiatrist. Then she told me that she was seeing a psychiatrist, two plumbers and a lawyer.

If Gregor Mendel had been alive today, he would have won the Nobel Peas Prize.

Great One Liners

What's green and sits in the corner?
The Incredible Sulk.

What can you serve, but not eat?
A tennis ball.

Who killed all the fish in the sea? Billy the Squid.
Who killed Billy the Squid? Jack the Kipper.
Who killed Jack the Kipper? The Codfather.

All I got for my birthday this year was a pack of sticky cards. I found it very hard to deal with.

I read somewhere that 77% of the mentally ill live in poverty. Actually, I'm more intrigued by the 23% who are apparently doing all right.

Anything not nailed down is a cat toy.

Why do mice have such tiny balls? Because so few of them can dance.

What's the difference between erotic and kinky? Erotic, you use a feather. Kinky, you use the whole chicken.

What are the most common last words of a redneck? "Hey, y'all, watch this!"

Bad breath is better than no breath at all.

I'm an apathetic sociopath. I'd kill you if I cared.

I need not suffer in silence while I can still moan, whimper and complain.

When someone hurts me, forgiveness is cheaper than a lawsuit. But not nearly as gratifying.

I am learning that criticism is not nearly as effective as sabotage.

Someday, we'll look back on this and plow into a parked car.

I was the next door kid's imaginary friend.

What do you call bears without ears? "B"

Next time you wave, use all your fingers.

I may not be totally perfect, but parts of me are excellent.

I have abandoned my search for truth and am now looking for a good fantasy.

THINGS MY MOTHER TAUGHT ME:

...ABOUT RELIGION. "You better pray that will come out of the carpet."

...TIME TRAVEL. "If you don't straighten up, I'm going to knock you into the middle of next week!"

...LOGIC. "Because I said so, that's why."

...FORESIGHT. "Make sure you wear clean underwear in case you're in an accident."

...IRONY. "Keep crying and I'll give you something to cry about."

...STAMINA. "You'll sit there until all that spinach is gone."

...WEATHER. "This room of yours looks like a tornado went though it.

..BEHAVIOR CHANGE. "Stop acting like Dad."

...ENVY. "There are millions of children in the world who don't have wonderful parents like us."

...ANTICIPATION. "Just wait 'til we're home!"

...MEDICAL SCIENCE. "If you keep crossing your eyes, your face with freeze that way."

...ESP. "Put your sweater on. I know that you'll be cold if you don't."

...GENETICS. "You're just like your father."

...HOW TO BECOME AN ADULT. "If you don't eat your veggies, you'll never grow up."

......WISDOM. "When you get to be my age, you'll understand."

...SHARING. "I'm going to give you a piece of my mind."

...FEAR. "One day I hope you'll have a child just like you."

I feel much better, now that I've given up hope.

I try to take one day at a time ... but sometimes several days attack me at once.

All I want is a warm bed, a kind word, and unlimited power.

Great One Liners

Appreciate me now, and avoid the rush.

How can you tell a macho woman?
She rolls her own tampons.

Why does a chicken coop have two doors?
Because if it had four doors, it would be a chicken sedan.

Q: why is divorce so expensive?
A: because it's worth it.

Current death rate: one per person.

Two wrongs are only the beginning.

I hope that life isn't just one big joke because I don't get it.

Drugs may lead nowhere, but at least it's a scenic route.

Incompatibility can be a good thing. The man has income and the woman is pattable.

If you must choose between two evils, pick the one you've never tried before.

To vacillate or not to vacillate, that is the question. Or is it?

How many lawyers does it take to shingle a roof? One, if you slice him thin enough.

THREE PROOFS JESUS WAS PUERTO RICAN:
His first name was Jesus.
He was always in trouble with the law.
His mother didn't know who his father was.

THREE PROOF JESUS WAS JEWISH
He went into his father's business.
He lived at home until age 33.
He was sure his mother was a virgin and she was sure he was God.

THREE PROOFS THAT JESUS WAS IRISH
He never got married.
He never held a steady job.
His last request was a drink.

THREE PROOFS THAT JESUS WAS ITALIAN
He talked with his hands.
He had wine with every meal.
He worked in the building trades.

THREE PROOFS THAT JESUS WAS BLACK
He called everybody brother.
He had no permanent address.
Nobody would hire him.

Great One Liners

Stupid? I don't know the meaning of the word.

How are a Texas tornado and a Tennessee divorce the same? Somebody's gonna lose a trailer

Welcome to Delaware–Only 15 more miles to New Jersey.

Welcome to Alabama–Place redneck joke here.

Welcome to W. Virginia-Our family trees may not fork, but our roads sure as hell do.

Welcome to Missouri–We have ways of making your mispronounce the letter "I".

Welcome to N. Carolina–Thank you for smoking.

Welcome to Hawaii–How the hell did you drive here?

Welcome to Texas–where all 5'2" women are 5'7".

Welcome to Mississippi–Our children is learning to read.

How did Hitler die? He saw his gas bill.

Great One Liners

I know an archeologist whose career is in ruins.

Why do scuba divers fall backwards into the water? If they fell frontwards, they'd be in the boat.

To err is human, to arr is pirate.

Beauty parlor: a place where women curl up and dye.

Chickens: the only animals you eat before they are born and after they die.

Yawn: an honest opinion, openly expressed.

Handkerchief: cold storage.

Tomorrow: one of the greatest labor-saving devices of today.

Inflation: cutting money in half without damaging the paper.

My whole purpose in life is to serve as a warning to others.

Being poor sure takes up a lot of a person's time.

WELCOME TO THE PSYCHIATRIC HOTLINE

If you have multiple personalities, please press 3,4,5, and 6.

If you are obsessive-compulsive, please press 1 repeatedly.

If you are co-dependent, please ask someone to press 2.

If you are paranoid-delusional, we know who you are and what you want. Just stay on the line so we can trace the call.

If you are schizophrenic, listen carefully and a little voice will tell you which number to press.

If you are manic-depressive, it doesn't matter which number you press. No one will answer.

If you are delusional and occasionally hallucinate, please be aware that the thing you are holding on the side of your head is alive and about to bite off your ear.

If you are a depressive, don't press anything Just sit there and cry.

You can't pin anything on a nudist.

She's not easy, just horizontally accessible.

She doesn't sag; she's only gravitationally challenged.

He's not a bad dancer; he's over Caucasian.

She's not unsophisticated, just socially challenged.

He's not a sex machine; he is romantically automated.

He does not hog the blankets; he is thermally unappreciative.

He is not a male chauvinistic pig; he has Swine Empathy.

She does not eat like a pig; she suffers from Reverse Bulimia.

He does not undress you with his eyes; he has an introspective pornographic moment.

She was increasingly worried and concerned about the lack of anxiety in her life.

Why is truth called naked and not nude?

She might have been a Marine colonel's daughter, but she was rotten to the corps.

Forget getting high in Hawaii. There, you only get aloha.

Great One Liners

My cat sucks lemons, the sourpuss.

If being in fashion is so desirable, why does it change so often?

What makes the universe so easy to comprehend is that there are so many things out there for comparisons.

Remember, in the game of life, a 44 Magnum always beats 4 aces.

That's the story of my life. Trying to remember where I'm at.

I knew she was an embalmer's daughter when she left me completely drained.

The future is much like the present, but considerably longer.

Them that has, gets and then gets away with it.

Military justice is to justice as military music is to music.

Yield to temptation. It may not come your way again.

Things are more like they used to be than they are now.

Misfortune: the kind of fortune that never misses.

Nudists are limited to one-button suits.

So narrow-minded, she could see through keyholes with both eyes.

If you yelled at your plants, instead of talking, would they grow troubled and insecure?

Why do people with closed minds always open their mouths?

If you mixed vodka with orange juice and milk of magnesia, would you get a Phillips Screwdriver?

When you hear the toilet flush followed by the words "Uh-oh" it's already too late.

A dyslexic sold his soul to Santa.

No matter how much Jello you put into the bathtub, you still can't walk on water.

I refuse to star in your psychodrama.

How does a spoiled rich girl change a lightbulb?
She asks Daddy for a new apartment.

IN THE STOCK MARKET TODAY:

Helium was up.
Feathers were down and paper was stationery.
Weights were up in heavy trading.
Fluorescent tubes were down in light trading.
Light switches were off.
Caterpillar stock inched up a bit.
Knives were up sharply.
Cows were steered into a bull market.
Pencils were down a few points.
Hiking equipment was trailing.
Elevators were up.
Escalators experienced a slight decline.
Mining equipment hit rock bottom.
Diapers were unchanged.
Prunes plummeted.
Sun peaked at midday.
Balloon prices were inflated.
There was heavy trading of metals
The bottom fell out of disposable diapers.
Major shipping lines stayed on an even keel.
Pain relievers sored.

Me? Uniquely maladjusted, but fun.

I have a PBS mind in an MTV world.

I had a dyslexic girlfriend in Idaho who wrote me a John Deere letter.

Do illiterate people get the full effect of alphabet soup?

How do you drive an engineer completely insane? Tie him to a chair, stand in front of him, and fold up a road map the wrong way.

The face is familiar, but I can't quite remember my name.

It's been lovely, but I have to scream now.

A fool and his money are soon partying.

Ambition is a poor excuse for not having enough sense to be lazy.

If procrastinators had a club, would they ever have a meeting?

If you crossed a chicken with a zebra would you get a 4-legged chicken with its own bar code?

Great One Liners

If time heals all wounds, how come the belly button stays the same?

Just one letter makes all the difference between here and there.

Men know that cats are evil and can't be trained.

Men know how to change the toilet paper, but to do so would ruin the game.

Men know that men are from here and woman are from way the hell over there.

It's easy to identify people who can't count to ten. They're in front of you in the supermarket express lane.

Take comedians seriously and politicians as a joke.

I see you've set aside this special time to humiliate yourself in public.

Marriage is the triumph of imagination over intelligence.
Second marriage is the triumph of hope over experience.

I drink to make other people interesting.

What are you up to?
My ideal weight if I were 11 feet tall.

MORE CLASSIC WOODY ALLEN
A man goes to a psychiatrist and says, "My brother's crazy. He thinks he's a chicken." The doctor says, "Why don't you turn him in?" The guys says, "We would, but we need the eggs."

And in all of Babylonia there was wailing and gnashing of teeth, until the prophets bade the multitudes get a grip on themselves and shape up.

I'd call him a sadistic, hippophilic necrophile, but that would be beating a dead horse.

I ran into Isosceles, he had a great idea for a triangle.

The government is unresponsive to the needs of the little man. Under 5'7", it is impossible to get your congressman on the phone.

I'm very proud of my gold watch. My grandfather, on his death bed, sold me this watch.

On a butcher's window: "Let me meat your needs."

DIFFERENT DEFINITIONS

Giraffiti: vandalism spray-painted very very high.

Tatyr: a lecherous Mr. Potato Head

Foreploy: any misrepresentation about yourself for the purpose of obtaining sex.

Sarchasm: the gulf between the author of sarcastic wit and the recipient who doesn't get it.

Inoculatte: to take coffee intravenously, when you are running late.

Hipatitis: Terminal coolness (like, groovy, man.)

Glibido: all talk and no action.

Intaxication: euphoria at getting a tax refund.

Osteopornosis: a degenerate disease.

If brains were taxed, he'd get a rebate.

Do fish get thirsty?

Men would follow him anywhere, but only out of morbid curiosity.

What do you get when you put Spice Girls in the toaster? Pop Tarts.

He's a prime candidate for natural deselection.

He donated his brain to science before he was done using it.

She has a room-temperature IQ.

On a dry cleaner's window: "Drop your pants here."

On the desk in a reception room: "We shoot every 3rd salesman and the 2nd one just left."

CLASSIC BOB HOPE
You know you're getting old when the candles cost more than the cake.

I have a wonderful make-up crew. They're the same people restoring the Statue of Liberty.

Middle age is when you still believe you'll feel better in the morning.

I grew up with six brothers. That's how I learned to dance–waiting for the bathroom.

A James Cagney love scene is where he lets the other guy live.

I do benefits for all religions. I'd hate to blow the hereafter on a technicality.

Zsa Zsa Gabor got married the first time and it was so successful she turned it into a series.

If you watch a game, it's fun. If you play it, it's recreation. If you work at it, it's golf.

Middle age is when your age begins to show around your middle.

I grew up with six brothers. That's how I learned to dance—waiting for the bathroom.

My father told me all about the birds and the bees, the liar. I went steady with a woodpecker until I was 21.

People who throw kisses are hopelessly lazy.

She said she was approaching 40 and I couldn't help wondering from which direction.

Where do mummies swim? In the Dead Sea.

Great One Liners

I love a martini, two at the most.
Two, I'm under the table.
Three, I'm under the host.
-Dorothy Parker

In Fairbanks, Alaska, it is illegal to give beer to a moose.

Sign in a cafeteria: "Shoes are required to eat in the cafeteria. Socks can eat anyplace they want."

I honor my personality flaws, for without them, I would have no personality at all.

Who can I blame for my problems? Give me just a minute ... I'll find someone.

As I learn the innermost secrets of the people around me, they reward me in many ways to keep me quiet.

Joan of Arc heard voices, too.

I have the power to channel my imagination into ever-soaring levels of suspicion and paranoia.

Sign in a restaurant window: "Don't stand there and be hungry. Come in and get fed up."

Great One Liners

Never go to bed mad. Stay up and fight.
-Phyllis Diller

Anger is only one letter short of danger.

I must confess, I was born at an early age.

How do you get a Kentucky graduate off your porch? Pay for the pizza.

She's got more chins than the Hong Kong telephone directory.

She got her good looks from her father. He's a plastic surgeon.

My boss's idea of an unnatural act is giving someone a raise.

Don't confuse fame with success. Madonna is one; Helen Keller is the other.
-Erma Bombeck

Never miss the chance to shut up.

A committee keeps minutes and loses hours.

Love means telling you why you're sorry.

Great One Liners

WOMEN'S COMEBACKS TO BAD PICKUP LINES:

Man: Haven't I seen you someplace before?
Woman: That's why I don't go there anymore.

Man: Is this seat empty?
Woman: Yes, and this one, too, if you sit down.

Man: So, wanna go back to my place?
Woman: I dunno. Will two people fit under a rock?

Man: I know how to please a woman.
Woman: Then please leave me alone.

Man: So, what do you do for a living?
Woman: I'm a female impersonator.

Man: I want to give myself to you.
Woman: Sorry, I don't accept cheap gifts.

CLASSIC DOROTHY PARKER

I'm never going to be famous. My name will never be writ large on the roster of Those Who Do Things. I don't do any thing. Not one single thing. I used to bite my nails, but I don't even do that anymore.

I might repeat to myself slowly and soothingly, a list of quotations beautiful, from minds profound..If I can remember any of the damn things.

I don't care what is written about me just so long as it isn't true.

I don't know much about being a millionaire, but I'll bet I'd be darling at it.

If the girls who attended the Yale Prom were laid end to end, it wouldn't surprise me at all.

This is not a novel to be tossed aside lightly. It should be thrown with great force.

Oh, life is a glorious cycle of song/A medley of extemporanea/ And love is a thing that can never go wrong/and I am the Queen of Romania.

Trapped, like a trap in a trap.

There's a helluva distance between wisecracking and wit. Wit has truth in it; wisecracking is simply calisthenics with words.

Men seldom make passes/At girls who wear glasses.

The two most beautiful words in the English language are "check enclosed."

The best way to keep children at home is to make the home atmosphere pleasant–and let the air out of the tires.

This would be a good thing for them to cut on my tombstone: Wherever she went, including here, it was against her better judgement.

Marriage has no guarantees. If that's what you're looking for, go live with a car battery.

She's like an old shoe. Everything's worn out but the tongue.

Always remember: one good turn gets most of the blankets.

Marriage: an expensive way to get your laundry done for free.

Love many, trust few, and always paddle your own canoe.

Misery doesn't love company...nowadays, it insists upon it.

I think, therefore I'm single.

Great One Liners

If you love something, turn it loose. If it doesn't come back, hunt it down and kill it.

Marriage means commitment. Of course, so does insanity.

Early to bed, early to rise, and your girlfriend goes out with other guys.

Love is a merry little elf who dances a jig, then turns on you with a machine gun.

He broke my heart... so I broke his jaw.

I ran into my ex the other day, then hit reverse and ran into him again.

Marriage isn't a word. It's a sentence.

Sex: the pleasure is momentary, the position ridiculous, and the expense damnable.

My idea of housework is to sweep the room with a glance.

Junk is something you've kept for years and throw away three weeks before you need it.

Great One Liners

Age is a very high price to pay for maturity.

Men are from earth, women are from earth. Deal with it.

—— No husband has ever been shot while doing the dishes.

Opportunities always look bigger going than coming.

Eat healthy, stay fit, die anyway.

If you look like your passport picture, you probably need the trip.

For every action, there is an equal and opposite government program.

It is easier to get forgiveness than permission.

There is not one shred of evidence that supports the notion that life is serious.

Middle age is when broadness of the mind and narrowness of the waist change places.

Thou shalt not weigh more than thy refrigerator.

Blessed are they who can laugh at themselves for they shall never cease to be amused.

There is always one more imbecile than you counted on.

If necessity is the mother of invention, how come so many unnecessary things are invented?

Someone who thinks logically provides a nice contrast to the real world.

By the time you can make ends meet, they move the ends.

Does killing time damage eternity?

Do pilots take crash courses?

Do stars clean themselves with meteor showers?

Why is it that night falls, but day breaks.

Are part-time band leaders semi-conductors?

Can you buy a complete chess set in a pawn shop?

Have you ever seen a toad on a toadstool?

Daylight Savings Time. Why are they saving it and where are they keeping it?

How many weeks are there in a light year?

A child of five would understand this. Send someone to get a child of five.

I drink to make other people interesting.

How would you like to feel the way she looks?

A moose is an animal with horns on the front of its head and a hunting-lodge wall on the back.

Funny, I've met a lot of pin-up girls, but I've never been able to pin one down.

I have nothing but confidence in you ... and very little of that.

Go, and never darken my towels again.

Anyone who says he can see through women is missing a lot.

Why do the signs that say "Slow Children" have a picture of a running child?

If you shouldn't drink and drive, why do bars have parking lots?

If tin whistles are made of tin, what are fog horns made of?

Why do they call it chili if it's hot?

A man is only as old as the woman he feels.

Do you think I can buy back my introduction to you?

A hospital bed is a parked taxi with the meter running.

If you want to see a comic strip, come see me in the shower.

Laugh and the world laughs with you. Cry, and you're probably watching the wrong channel.

It isn't necessary to have relatives in Kansas City in order to be unhappy.

Nobody is completely unhappy at the failure of his best friend.

I wouldn't belong to any club that would accept me as a member.
-Groucho Marx

Wives are people who feel they don't dance enough.

The only game I like to play is Old Maid, providing she's not too old.

Those are my principles, and if you don't like them ... well, I have others.

There's one thing I want to do before I quit ... retire.

Outside of a dog, a book is man's best friend. Inside of a dog, it's too dark to read.

Paying alimony is like feeding hay to a dead horse.

You're from Wales? Do you a guy named Jonah? He lived there for awhile.

Women should be obscene and not heard.

All humans are born alike – except Democrats and Republicans.

You have the brain of a four-year-old and I'll bet he was glad to get rid of it.

You're heading for a breakdown, why don't you pull yourself to pieces?

Wife: I was a fool when I married you.
Husband: Yes, dear, but I was in love and didn't notice.

There's no middle ground with this guy—you either hate him or detest him.

She may be a vegetarian but she's still full of baloney.

He has the grace of a swan, the wisdom of an owl, the eye of an eagle...ladies and gentlemen, this man is for the birds!

Support group: cocktail hour with the girls.

MORE CLASSIC ERMA BOMBECK

I am not a glutton. I am an explorer of food.

A friend never defends a husband who gets his wife an electric skillet for her birthday.

I come from a family where gravy is considered a beverage.

I will not participate in any sport with ambulances at the bottom of a hill.

If you can't make it better, you can laugh at it.

A child develops individuality long before he develops taste. I've seen my kid straggle into the kitchen in the morning with outfits that need only one accessory: an empty gin bottle.

When humor goes, there goes civilization.

In two decades I've lost a total of 789 pounds. I should be hanging from a charm bracelet.

There's nothing sadder in the world than to awake Christmas morning and not be a child.

Parenting is a negative thing. Keep your children from killing themselves or anyone else, and hope for the best.

Thanksgiving dinners take 18 hours to prepare. They are consumed in 12 minutes. Half-times are 12 minutes long. This is not a coincidence.

Never lend your car to anyone to whom you have given birth.

Never go to a doctor whose office plants have died.

My second favorite household chore is ironing, my first being hitting my head on the top bunk bed until I faint.

PETER KAY, BRITISH HUMORIST

I was doing some decorating so I got out my step-ladder. I don't get along with my real ladder.

I saw six men kicking and punching the mother-in-law. My neighbor said, "Aren't you going to help?" I said, "No, six should be enough."

You know that look women get when they want sex? No? Well, neither do I.

I think animal testing is a terrible idea. They get all nervous and give the wrong answers.

How young can you die of old age?

If we aren't supposed to eat animals, then why are they made of meat?

My Dad used to say "always fight fire with fire," which is probably why he was kicked out of the fire brigade.

I went to a restaurant that said "Breakfast any time," so I ordered eggs during the Renaissance.

Studies show that 100% of those who advocate abortion are people who have already been born.

She can offer lots of advice, good advice, advice that's been passed down from generation to generation and never been used.

He went to a ballet once. He didn't like it. He couldn't even tell who won.

Have you ever wondered why the same candy bar that rots a child's teeth is a wonderful source of quick energy for adults?

I had a terrible childhood. I'm probably the only guy in history who was bitten by the Tooth Fairy.

Granola solves everything.

He's probably the only guy in town who ever got his finger caught in a screwdriver.

Great One Liners

Why should I pay $9.00 for a movie tickets when I can see the same movie on TV for $40 a month?

Remember, parents, never let your daughter take a purse to church large enough to hold a kitten.

If all the nations in the world are in debt, where did all the money go?

If you're a born-again, do you have two belly buttons?

Can you be arrested for selling illegal-sized paper?

Could crop circles be the work of a cereal killer?

Do good S&M fans go to Hell?

If vampires have no reflection, how come they have such neat hair?

If a person told you they were a pathological liar... would you believe them?

If God dropped acid, would He see people?

Can you learn to read from a "Reading for Dummies" book?

When dog food is new and improved and better tasting, who tests it?

Why can't women apply mascara with their mouths closed?

If a man washes a dish and no woman is around to see it, did it happen?

Why doesn't onomatopoeia sound like what it is?

Why exactly do they make snow globes with a summer scene?

Do three-headed fire dragons have heated arguments with themselves?

What do picket-sign writers put on their signs when they go on strike?

If we learn from mistakes, why am I not a genius?

Why don't people on tv programs ever go to the bathroom?

How do blind people know when they're done wiping?

Why do people order a double cheeseburger, double fries, and a diet coke?

How is it that "fat chance" and "slim chance" mean the same thing?

Who copyrighted the copyright system?

He who hesitates is probably right.

Did you ever notice that the Roman numerals for forty are XL?

If you think there is good in everybody, you haven't met everybody.

If you put "the" and "IRS" together, it spells "theirs."

Eventually, we reach the point where we stop lying about our age and start bragging about it.

The older we get, the fewer things seem worth waiting in line for.

When you are dissatisfied and would like to go back to your youth, think of Geometry.

Deja Moo: the feeling you've heard this bull before.

A penny saved is a government oversight.

Long ago, when men cursed and beat the ground with sticks, it was called witchcraft. Today, we know it as golf.

A man walks into a bar with a slab of asphalt under his arm and says: "A beer, please, and one for the road."

Daisy the cow says to her friend Dolly: "I was artificially inseminated today." "I don't believe you!" says Dolly. "It's true," says Daisy. "No bull!"

I went to buy some camouflage pants today, but I couldn't see any.

Last night, as I lay in bed looking at the stars, I thought, "Where in hell is the ceiling?"

In case of emergency, speak in cliches.

When the blind leadeth the blind, get out of the way.

Great One Liners

Strangers have the best candy.

Make the most of yourself, because that's all the self you are going to get, Mister.

I went to a general store. They wouldn't let me buy anything specific.

When in doubt, mumble.

There are two types of people, those who divide people into two types, and those who don't.

Give me liberty, or give me a bran muffin!

How many vegetables had to die to make your salad?

Bad spellers of the world, untie!

Writing about music is like dancing about architecture.

Poets have been curiously silent about cheese.

Give some folks an inch and they think they're rulers.

Great One Liners

It's all fun and games until someone loses a tooth … and then it's hockey!

Instant human. Just add coffee.

There is no I in team, but there is a ME.

Dancing is like a shower; one wrong turn and you're in hot water.

Go now, or forever hold your pee.

Anger the French. Make tacos.

Worry is the first time you can't do it a second time; panic is the second time you can't do it the first time.

I guess I am a better door than a window, even though you say I'm a pain.

I can't remember if I'm the good twin, or the evil one.

Diplomacy: the art of letting someone have your way.

Aspire to be Barbie; the bitch has everything.

If life deals you lemons, make lemonade. If it deals you tomatoes, make Bloody Marys. But if it deals you a truckload of hand grenades ... now THAT'S a message!

Anything free is worth what you pay for it.

Better living though denial.

Do not disturb. Already disturbed.

Does the name Pavlov ring a bell?

Eat lamb. 50,000 coyotes can't be wrong.

Feel lucky? Update your software.

MORE CLASSIC GEORGE CARLIN

Honesty may be the best policy, but it's important to remember that apparently, by elimination, dishonesty is the second-best policy.

I don't like to think of laws as rules you have to follow, but more as suggestions.

Eventually, alas, I realized the main purpose of buying cocaine is to run out of it.

I love and treasure individuals as I meet them; I loathe and despise the groups they identify with and belong to.

Don Ho can sign autographs 3.4 times faster than Efrem Zimbalist Jr.

The reason they call it the American Dream is because you have to be asleep to believe it.

Most people work just hard enough not to get fired and get paid just enough money not to quit.

When you think about it, attention-deficit order makes a lot of sense. In this country, there isn't a lot worth paying attention to.

The very existence of flamethrowers proves that some time, somewhere, someone said to themselves: "You know, I want to set those people over there on fire, but I 'm just not close enough to get the job done."

I let my mind wander and it never came back.

The Golden Gate Bridge should have a long bungee cord for people who aren't quite ready to commit suicide but want to get in a little practice.

Great One Liners

I have as much authority as the Pope. I just don't have as many people who believe it.

I don't have a fear of heights. I do, however, have a fear of falling from heights.

Kilometers are shorter than miles. Save gas. Take your next trip in kilometers.

"No comment" is a comment.

Why is the alphabet in that order? Is it because of that song?

The real reason we can't have the Ten Commandments in a courthouse: You cannot post "Thou shalt not steal," "Thou shalt not commit adultery," and "Thou shalt not lie" in a building full of lawyers, judges, and politicians. It creates a hostile work environment.

I killed a 6-pack just to watch it die.

Where are we going? And what's with this hand basket?

If a man smiles all the time, he's probably selling something that doesn't work.

I'm not into working out. My philosophy is no pain, no pain.

Never raise your hand to your kids. It leaves your groin unprotected.

I want revenge. Is that so wrong?

I had a life once. Now I have a computer and a modem.

So far, this is the oldest I've been.

I don't believe it. I failed my urine test.

I don't suffer from stress. I'm a carrier.

I don't care. I don't have to.

I don't care who you are, Fatso! Get your reindeer off my roof!

I don't have a license to kill but I do have a learner's permit.

I don't find it hard to meet expenses. They're everywhere.

Doctor: You'll live to be 60.
Patient: I <u>am</u> sixty.
Doctor: See? What did I tell you?

I need someone really bad. Are you really bad?

I didn't have a penny to my name so I changed my name.

I tried switching to gum, but it wouldn't stay lit.

I tried to think, but nothing happened.

I support the three basic food groups: keg... bottle ... can.

I still miss my ex, but my aim is getting better.

I smile because I'm totally clueless.

I said "no" to drugs, but they wouldn't listen.

Tell me to "stuff it." I'm a taxidermist.

The life of a $50 bill is six months. How come I've never had one die in my hands?

I won't rise to the occasion but I'll slide to it.

Tell me what you need, and I'll tell you how to get along without it.

The two most common elements in the universe are hydrogen and stupidity.

The 50-50-90 rule: Anytime you have a 50-50 chance of getting something right, there's a 90% probability you'll get it wrong.

The shop called yesterday, your brain is ready.

The Religious Right is neither.

The older I get, the better I was.

The proctologist called; they found your head.

The only cure for insomnia is to get more sleep.

Beatings will continue until morale improves.

The more I know about women, the more I love my truck.

The way to get things done is not to care who gets the credit.

This isn't Burger King. You can't have it your way.

If I save the whales, where do I keep them?

If the shoe fits, get another one just like it.

If we do not succeed, then we run the risk of failure.
   -Dan Quayle

If I save time, when do I get it back?

NEW WORDS FROM THE WASHINGTON POST:

Abdicate: to give up all hope of ever having a flat stomach.

Balderdash: a rapidly receding hairline.

Bustard: a very rude Metro bus driver.

Carcinoma: a valley in California notable for its heavy smog.

Circumvent: the opening in a pair of boxer shorts.

Coffee: a person who is coughed upon.

Decafalon: getting through the day drinking and eating only things that are good for you.

Esplanade: to attempt an explanation while drunk.

Flabbergasted: appalled over how much weight you've gained.

Flatulence: the emergency vehicle that picks you up after you are run over by a steamroller.

Gargoyle: an olive-flavored mouthwash.

Negligent: describes a condition in which you absentmindedly answer the door in your nightie.

Oyster: a person who sprinkles his conversation with Yiddish expressions.

Pokemon: a Jamaican proctologist.

Rectitude: the formal, dignified demeanor assumed by a proctologist immediately before he examines you.

Frisbeetarianism: the belief that when you die, your soul goes up on the roof and gets stuck there.

WHAT DO YOU GET WHEN YOU CROSS...

...a banana with a red silk dress? A pink slip.

...a canary with a mole? A miner bird.

...a cat with a lemon? A sourpuss.

...a chicken with a bell? An alarm cluck.

...a dog with a cantaloupe? A melon-collie baby.

...a dog with a chicken? A hen that lays pooched eggs.

...a dog with a daisy? A collie-flower.

...a dove with a high chair? A stool pigeon.

...a duck with a steamroller? A flat duck.

...a fawn with a hornet? Bambee.

...a gorilla and a sheep? A very nice wool coat, except the sleeves are too long.

...a ham with a karate expert? Pork chops.

...a hedgehog and a snake? Two yards of barbed wire.

...a hummingbird with a doorbell? A humdinger.

...a movie with a swimming pool a dive-in theater.

...a parrot with a centipede? A walkie-talkie.

...a pig with a cactus? A porkerpine.

...a pit bull with a collie? A dog that bites your leg off and runs for help.

...a policeman with a telegram? Copper wire.

...a potato with an onion? A potato with watery eyes.

...a rabbit with a kilt? Hopscotch.

...a spider with a rabbit? A hare net.

...a termite with a house? An exterminator.

...a tiger with a needle? Pin stripes.

...a tree with a baseball player? Babe Root.
...a vulture with a small grass house? A scavenger hut.
...an Eskimo with a pig? A polar boar.
...an Indian with a cow? Geronimoo.
...an evangelist with a hockey puck? A puck that saves itself.
...an owl with a goat? A hootenanny.
...a farmer with Robin Hood? A hoe bow.
...an elephant with a frisbee? A hernia.
...an ant with an elephant? A dead ant.
...a skunk with an elephant? Very few friends.
...an elephant with a skin doctor? A pachydermatologist.
...a dairy cow with an elephant? Peanut butter.
...an elephant with a rhino? Elephino.

A man needs a mistress just to break the monogamy.

A plateau is a high form of flattery.

Condoms should be used in every conceivable occasion.

Dancing cheek-to-cheek is really a form of floor play.

Local Area Network in Australia: the LAN down under.

Marathon runners with bad shoes suffer the agony of de feet.

Reading while sunbathing makes you well red.

She was engaged to a boy with a wooden leg but broke it off.

Shotgun wedding: a case of wife or death.

Those who get too big for their britches will be exposed in the end.

To write with a broken pencil is pointless.

Astronomers say the universe is finite, which is a comforting thought for those people who can't remember where they leave things.

In the beginning, the Universe was created. This has made a lot of people very angry and been widely regarded as a bad move.
-Douglas Adams

My theology, briefly, is that the universe was dictated but not signed.
-Christopher Morley

The universe is a big place, perhaps the biggest.

The surest sign that intelligent life exists elsewhere in the universe is that it has never tried to contact us.
-Calvin and Hobbes

When two egoists meet, it's an I for an I.

When you do a good deed, get a receipt in case Heaven is like the IRS.

You can't be first, but you could be next.

You can tune a guitar but you can't tunafish.

Winning isn't everything; it's also important to humiliate your opponent.

Who are these kids and why are they calling me Mom?

Why are there so many Smiths in the phone book? They all have phones.

668: the neighbor of The Beast.

Madness takes its toll. Please have exact change.

A Freudian slip is when you say one thing but mean your mother.

Karate is a form of martial arts in which people who have had years and years of training can, using only their hands and feet, make some of the worst movies in the history of the world.
    -Dave Barry

With every passing hour our solar system comes 43,000 miles closer to globular cluster M13 in the constellation Hercules; and still there are some misfits who continue to insist that there is no such thing as progress.
    -Ransom K. Ferm

"My sister is a waitress in a mental hospital."
"What does she do?"
"She serves soup to nuts."

May the forces of evil become confused on the way to your house.
    -George Carlin

Life may have no meaning. Or even worse, it may have a meaning of which I disapprove.
    -Ashleigh Brilliant

Los Angeles is the home of the three little white lies: "The Ferrari is paid for," "The mortgage is assumable," and "It's only a cold sore."

Drawing on my fine command of language, I said nothing.

Her kisses left something to be desired–the rest of her.

Always try to do things in chronological order; it's less confusing that way.

For three days after death, hair and fingernails continue to grow but phone calls taper off.
-Johnny Carson

Gladstone to Disraeli: I predict, sir, that you will die either by hanging or of some vile disease.
Disraeli to Gladstone: That all depends, sir, upon whether I embrace you principles or your mistress.

When I told the people of Northern Ireland that I was an atheist, a woman in the audience stood up and said, "Yes, but is it the God of the Catholics or the God of the Protestants in whom you don't believe?"
-Quentin Crisp

Lazlo's Chinese Relativity Axiom: No matter how great your triumphs or how tragic your defeats–approximately one billion Chinese couldn't care less.

I think that the team that wins game five will win the series. Unless we lose game five.

Sorry, but my karma just ran over your dogma.

Based on what you know about him in history books, what do you think Abraham Lincoln would be doing if he were alive today?
1. Writing his memoirs of the Civil War.
2. Advising the President
3. Desperately clawing at the inside of his coffin.
    -David Letterman

I think that all right-thinking people in this country are sick and tired of being told that ordinary, decent people are fed up in this country with being sick and tired. I'm certainly not! But I'm sick and tired of being told that I am!
    -Monty Python

Experience is that marvelous thing that enables you to recognize a mistake when you make it again.
    -F. P. Jones

Some mornings, it's just not worth chewing through the leather straps.
-Emo Phillips

Those who make peaceful revolution impossible will make violent revolution inevitable.
-John F. Kennedy

Sometimes I lie awake at night and I ask, "Where have I gone wrong?" Then a voice says to me, "This is going to take more than one night."
–Charlie Brown, Peanuts

The only difference between me and a madman is that I am not mad.
-Salvadore Dali

I hate to advocate drugs, alcohol, violence, or insanity to anyone; but they've always worked for me.
-Hunter S. Thompson

What a distressing contrast there is between the radiant intelligence of a child and the feeble mentality of the average adult.
-Sigmund Freud

Speak softly and carry a cell phone.

There's so much comedy on television. Does that cause comedy on the streets?
-Dick Cavett

Old Yiddish Proverb: If triangles had a God, he would have 3 sides.

Thou shalt not kill. Thou shalt not commit adultery. Don't eat pork. I'm sorry, what was that last one?? Don't eat pork? God has spoken. Is that the word of God or is that pigs trying to outsmart everybody?
-Jon Stewart

When I was a kid, I had two friends, and they were imaginary and they would only play with each other.
-Rita Rudner

I haven't taken my Christmas lights down. They look so nice on the pumpkin.
–Winston Spear

Beauty is only a light switch away.

I worry that the person who thought up Muzak may be thinking up something else.
-Lily Tomlin

My grandfather's a little forgetful, but he likes to give me advice. One day, he took me aside and left me there.
-Ron Richards

According to a new survey, women say they feel more comfortable undressing in front of men than they do undressing in front of other women. They say that women are too judgmental, where, of course, men are just grateful.
-Jay Leno

Where lipstick is concerned, the important thing is not color, but to accept God's final word on where your lips end.
-Jerry Seinfeld

I planted some bird seed. A bird came up. Now I don't know what to feed it.
-Stephen Wright

If God doesn't destroy Hollywood Boulevard, he owes Sodom and Gomorrah an apology.
-Jay Leno

You know how to tell if the teacher is hung over? Movie Day.
-Jay Mohr

I ask people why they have deer heads on their walls. They always say because it's such a beautiful animal. There you go. I think my mother is attractive, but I have photographs of her.
-Ellen deGeneres

Everything that used to be a sin is now a disease.
-Jay Mohr

Now they show you how detergents take out bloodstains, a pretty violent image there. I think if you've got a t-shirt with a bloodstain all over it, maybe laundry isn't your biggest problem. Maybe you should get rid of the body before you do the wash.
-Jerry Seinfeld

At the feast of ego, everyone leaves hungry.

In the last couple of weeks, I have seen the ads for the Wonder Bra. Is that really a problem in this country? Men not paying enough attention to women's breasts?
-Jay Leno

The psychiatrist said to his patient, "You really must give up smoking!" "Is it so bad for me?" asked the patient. "I don't know about that," said the doctor, "but you're burning holes in my couch."

Women need a reason to have sex. Men just need a place.
-Billy Crystal

If you can't beat them, arrange to have them beaten.
-George Carlin

Who won the skeleton contest? No body.
That married couples can live together day after day is a miracle that the Vatican has overlooked.
-Bill Cosby

Money can't buy everything ... but then again, neither can no money.

I love oral sex ... it's the phone bill I hate.

Men do not like to admit to even momentary imperfection. My husband forgot the code to turn off the alarm. When the police came, he wouldn't admit he'd forgotten the code ... he turned himself in.
-Rita Rudner

Men are liars. We'll lie about lying if we have to. I'm an algebra liar. I figure two good lies make a positive.
-Tim Allen

Doctors are reporting that latex condoms cause severe swelling. So what's the problem?
-Jay Leno

The problem with the designated driver program, it's not a desirable job. But if you ever get sucked into doing it, have fun with it. At the end of the night, drop them off at the wrong house.
-Jeff Foxworthy

After making love, I said to my girl, "So was it good for you, too?" She said, "I don't think this was good for anybody."
-Gary Shandling

We have women in the military but they don't put us in the front lines. They don't know if we can fight, if we can kill. I think we can. All the general has to do is walk over to the women and say, "You see the enemy over there? They say you look fat in your uniforms."
-Elayne Boosler

My mom said the only reason men are alive is for lawn care and vehicle maintenance.
-Tim Allen

If at first you don't succeed, I suggest you not play Russian Roulette.

If the good die young, what does that say about senior citizens?

The post office says they're raising the price of stamps by one cent because they need to upgrade their equipment. Apparently, they're going from semi-automatics to Uzis.
-Conan O'Brien

Men look at woman the way men look at cars. Everyone looks at Ferraris. Now and then we see a pickup truck and we all buy station wagons.
-Tim Allen

There's very little advice in men's magazines, because men don't think there's a lot they don't know. Women do. Women want to learn. Men think, "I know what I'm doing, just show me somebody naked."
-Jerry Seinfeld

What did the guitar say to the musician? "Pick on someone your own size!"

If voting could really change things, it would be illegal.

To do is to be. (Descartes) To be is to do. (Voltaire) Do be do be do. (Frank Sinatra)

God made pot. Man made beer. Who do you trust?

Women's rule of thumb: if it has tires or testicles, you're going to have trouble with it.

How does a nude show have a dress rehearsal?

Remember, it's not "How high are you?" It's "Hi, how are you?"

I've decided that to raise my grades, I must lower my standards.

An expert farmer is outstanding in his field.

Some river valleys are absolutely gorges.

We ought to rename Summer and call it Pride. Because pride goeth before a Fall.

The Irish government is always wealthy because the capital is Dublin.

In some places, fog will never be mist.

Never give your uncle an anteater.

What do you call a frightened diver? Chicken of the sea.

What goes up into the air white and comes down yellow and white? An egg.

What day of the year is a command to go forward? March 4th.

Plug a pizza in the socket and get a pizza delight.

What has four wheels and flies? A garbage truck.

The sheep rustler who broke out of jail is now on the lam.

Electronics of Biblical proportions: Solomon and Toshiba.

One day the wind stopped blowing in Chicago and everyone fell down.

You can spot a nomadic tree, when it packs its trunks and leaves.

How about the man who ran through a screen door? He strained himself.

Great One Liners

Hands are like bells, especially when wrung.

Did you hear about the optician? Two glasses and he made a spectacle of himself.

How to tickle a rich girl? Gucci, Gucci, Gucci!

What did the painter say to the wall? "One more crack and I'll plaster you!"

Tired Army clothes: fatigues.

What did Tarzan say to his wife? "Jane, it's a jungle out there!"

A rabbit with fleas: Bugs Bunny.

What color is a belch: burple.

What did the alien dandelion say to the earth dandelion: "Take me to your weeder."

The city with the largest rodent population is Hamsterdam.

If a seagull flies over the sea, then I guess a bagel flies over the bay.

After Godzilla ate a 4-cylinder Datsun, he said, "Gosh, I coulda had a V-8!"

I never forget a face, but in your case I'll be glad to make an exception!
-Groucho Marx

The worst time to have a heart attack is during a game of charades.
-Demetri Martin

Race is just a pigment of the imagination.
-Glen Highland

I have nothing to declare except my genius!
-Oscar Wilde, to U.S. Customs

If it wasn't for pickpockets, I'd have no sex life at all.
-Rodney Dangerfield

Nothing is fool-proof to a sufficiently talented fool.

Adding in a dark Chinese restaurant: dim sum

Arbitrator: a cook who leaves Arby's to work at McDonald's.

Avoidable: what a bullfighter tries to do.

Baloney: where some hemlines fall.

Bernadette: the act of torching a mortgage.

Burglarize: what a crook sees with.

Control: a short, ugly inmate.

Counterfeiters: workers who put together kitchen cabinets.

Eclipse: what a Cockney barber does.

Eyedropper: a clumsy ophthalmologist.

Heroes: what a guy in a boat does.

Left Bank: what the robber did when his bag was full of loot.

Paradox: two physicians.

Parasites: what you see from the top of the Eiffel Tower.

Pharmacist: helper on the farm.

Polarize: what penguins see with.

Primate: removing your spouse from in front of the television.

Relief: what trees do in Spring.

Rubberneck: what you do to relax your wife.

Seamstress: describes 250 pounds in a size 6.

Selfish: what the owner of a seafood store does.

Subdued: a guy who works on a submarine.

Sudafed: sued a government official.

Always go to other peoples' funerals, or they won't go to yours.

Did you hear about the computer programmer who starved to death in the shower? The shampoo directions said, "Wash, rinse, repeat."

My husband and I didn't sign a pre-nuptial agreement. We signed a mutual suicide pact.
    -Roseanne Barr

My grandmother was a very tough woman. She buried three husbands, and two of them were just napping.
-Rita Rudner

What does a vampire fear most?
Tooth decay.

A story about a pony on the pampas could be called "Little Horse on the Prairie."

Have you got bills to pay? Please give it back. He looks so silly bald.

MEDICAL TERMINOLOGY FOR THE LAYMAN
Anally: occurring every year
Antibody: against everyone
Artery: the study of fine paintings
Bacteria: back door to a cafeteria
Bandages: The Rolling Stones
Barium: what you do when CPR fails
Benign: what you be after you be eight
Botulism: tendency to make mistakes
Bowel: letters like A, E, I,O,U
Caesarean Section: a district in Rome
Cardiology: advanced study of poker playing
Cat Scan: searching for one's lost kitty
Cauterize: made eye contact with her

Colic: a sheep dog

Coma: a punctuation mark

Congenital: friendly

Cortizone: the local courthouse

D & C: where Washington is

Diarrhea: joural of daily events

Dilate: to live longer

Enema: not a friend

Enteritis: a penchant for burglary

ER: the things on your head that you hear with

Fester: quicker

Fibrillate: to tell lies

Fibula: a small lie

Gene: blue denim pants

Genital: non-Jewish

G.I. Series: baseball games between soldiers

Grippe: what you do to a suitcase

Hangnail: a coat hook

Hemorrhoid: a male from outer space

Herpes: what women do in the ladies' room

Hormones: what a prostitute does when she isn't paid.

ICU: peek-a-boo

Impotent: distinguished, well-known

Inpatient: tired of waiting

Intense pain: torture in a teepee

Labor pain: hurt at work

Medical staff: a doctor's cane

Minor operation: somebody else's

Morbid: a higher offer

Nitrate: lower than day rate

Node: was aware of

Organic: church musician

Organ transplant: what you do to your piano when you move.

Outpatient: a person who has fainted

Paralyze: two far-fetched stories

Pap smear: fatherhood test

Pathological: a reasonable way to go

Pelvis: cousin of Elvis

Pharmacist: person who makes a living dealing in agriculture

Plaster cast: the drunk roadies backstage at a rock concert

Post-operative: a mail deliverer

Prostate: flat on your back

Protein: in favor of young people

Recovery room: place to upholster furniture

Rectum: damn near killed him

Red blood count: Dracula

Rheumatic: amorous

Saline: where you go on your boyfriend's boat

Scar: rolled tobacco leaf

Secretion: hiding anything

Seizure: Roman emperor

Serology: study of English knighthood

Surgery: a reason to get an uninterruptable power supply

Sterile solution: not using the elevator during a fire

    Tablet: a small table

    Terminal illness: getting sick at the airport

    Tibia: country in North Africa

    Tumor: an extra pai

Urine: opposite of "you're out!"

Varicose: very close

Vein: conceited

When life gives you lemons, make lemonade and add vodka.

Why ambassadors never get sick: diplomatic immunity.

What jumps from cake to cake and smells of almonds? Tarzipan!

The gambler's heaven is Paradise.

A centrifuge is a hiding place for 100 people.

Deposed kings are throne away.

Illegally-parked frogs are toad away.

CLASSIC DAVE BARRY

Gravity is a contributing factor in nearly 73 percent of all accidents involving falling objects.

The leading cause of death among fashion models is falling through street grates.

I now realize that the small hills you see on ski slopes are formed around the bodies of 47-year-olds who tried to learn snowboarding.

The nuclear generator of brain sludge is television.

American consumers have no problem with carcinogens, but they will not purchase anything, including floor wax, that has fat in it.

The best baby-sitters, of course, are the baby's grandparents. You feel completely comfortable entrusting your baby to them for long periods, which is why most grandparents flee to Florida.

The problem with writing about religion is that you run the risk of offending sincerely religious people, and then they come after you with machetes.

Lead me not into temptation. I can find it myself.

Great One Liners

Americans who travel abroad for the first time are often shocked to discover that, despite all the progress that has been made in the last 50years, many foreign people still speak in foreign languages.

We parents must encourage our children to become educated, so they can get into a good college that we cannot afford.

We journalists make it a point to know very little about an extremely wide variety of topics; this is how we stay objective.

McDonald's gets its beef from Macau.

In 2 days, yesterday will be tomorrow.

If you want to say it with flowers, a single rose says, "I'm cheap."
-Delta Burke

"Doctor! Doctor! Sometimes I think I'm a tepee and some days I think I'm a wigwam!"
"Relax. You're two tents."

What's a 3-season bed? One without springs.

A cow eating grass is a lawn-mooer.

Meteorologists are a nervous lot because their future is always up in the air.

Writing is nature's way of letting you know how sloppy your thinking is.

I drove cross-country with a friend and we split the driving. We switched every half hour.

One morning my girlfriend asked me if I had slept well and I said no, I'd made a few mistakes.

I hate when my foot falls asleep during the day... that means it'll be up all night.

I have the oldest typewriter in the world. It types in pencil.

It's a thankless job but I have a lot of Karma to burn off.

I'm not being rude. You're just insignificant.

My wife and I tried to have breakfast together, but we had to stop of our marriage would have been wrecked.
    -Sir Winston Churchill

E.T. said to Phyllis Diller: "You look weird."

At an all-you-can-eat restaurant, is there a penalty for eating less than you can?

How come there's never a garage actually for sale at any garage sale?

If it ain't broke, fix it till it is.

If marriage were outlawed, then only outlaws would have in-laws.

Dijon-vu: the same mustard as before.

I always wanted to be a procrastinator, never got around to it.

My inferiority complex isn't as good as yours.

People will accept your ideas much more readily if you tell them Benjamin Franklin said it first.

Some folks are so dumb, they have to be watered twice a week.

I don't get even; I get odder.

Your mind isn't twisted as much as badly sprained.

It's income tax time again: time to gather up those receipts, get those tax forms, sharpen up that pencil, and stab yourself in the aorta.

Two goats are eating old movie film. The first goat says, "Pretty tasty, huh?" Says the second goat: "The book was better."

I went into my bank the other day and asked the teller to check my balance. She pushed me over!

Tourist: Have you lived here all your life?
Local: Not yet.

What happens to a lawyer when he takes Viagra? He gets taller.

What will a lawyer name his daughter? Sue.

I consider myself to be a pretty good judge of people. That's why I don't like any of them.
-Roseanne Barr

I love to sing and I love to drink scotch. Most people would rather listen to me drink scotch.
-George Burns

At my age, the happy hour is a nap.

A good time to keep your mouth shut is when you're in deep water.

No one has more driving ambition than the boy who wants to buy a car.

How come it takes so little time for the child who is afraid of the dark to become a teenager who wants to stay out all night?

Seat belts are not as confining as wheelchairs.

There are worse things than getting a wrong-number call at 4 AM. It could be a right number.

Be careful reading the fine print. There's no way you're going to like it.

Horrible to contemplate: in about 40 years, we'll have thousands of old ladies with tattoos.

I used to think you were a pain in the neck; but now my opinion of you is much lower.

BOSS: Are you good at filing?
PROSPECTIVE SECRETARY: Am I good at filing? Of course I'm good at filing. Just look at my nails!

He's got a lot of class - steerage!

They've discovered a food proven to reduce a woman's sex drive by 90%. Wedding cake.

We all know that the bread always lands butter side down. But if you have a toddler at home, you learn that it tastes pretty good.

Sometimes too much to drink isn't enough.

Nice to be here? At my age, it's nice to be anywhere.
-George Burns

HENNY YOUNGMAN CLASSICS

You have a ready wit. Let me know when it's ready.

I took my wife to a wife-swapping party. I had to throw in some cash.

My wife will buy anything marked down. She brought home two dresses and an escalator.

It's good to see you. It means you're not behind my back.

When my wife asked me to start a garden, the first thing I dug up was an excuse.

Why don't Jewish men drink? It interferes with their suffering.

There's a new Talking Jewish Mother doll. You pull the string and it says, "Again with the string?"

I think sex is better than logic, but I can't prove it.

A bra factory was robbed of thousands of dollars' worth of bras. My Dad says they could've prevented the robbery if they'd had a booby trap.

The second most-asked question in New York City is, "Are the Yankees going to win this year?" The most asked is, of course, "What the hell are you lookin' at?"

Hard work never killed anyone. But why take a chance?

A penny saved isn't much.

If at first you don't succeed, get new batteries.

Laugh and the world laughs with you. Cry and you have to blow your nose.

Parked illegally? Avoid parking tickets by leaving your wipers turned on to their maximum speed.

Inexpensive entertainment: during rush hour, sit in your parked car and point a hair dryer at passing cars. See if they slow down.

They're always holding hands. If they let go, they'll kill each other.

Life insurance payments keep me broke, but there's a silver lining in that cloud–when I die I'll be really rich!

The right to bear arms is only slightly less ludicrous than the right to arm bears.
-Chris Addison

Jesus is coming—and boy, is he pissed!

They say that if you line up all the cars in the world end to end, some idiot will try to pass them.

Insanity is hereditary; you get it from your kids.

In case of emergency, break glass. Scream. Bleed to death.

Impotence: nature's way of saying "no hard feelings."

If you don't like the way I drive, move off the sidewalk!

It's not just winning the game. It's drinking the beer.

I'm not as think as you drunk I am.

Just because I live in a house doesn't mean I'll clean it.

LET'S GET THE LAWYERS

What's the difference between God and a lawyer? God doesn't think He's a lawyer.

What are lawyers good for? They make used-car salesmen look good.

If a lawyer and an IRS agent were both drowning and you could save only one of them, would you go to lunch or read the paper?

What do lawyers and sperm have in common? It takes 300,000 of them of make one human being.

What do you call a lawyer gone bad? S

What do you throw to a drowning lawyer? His partners.

In the event of war, I'm a hostage.
-Woody Allen

Don't bite the hand that looks dirty.

Wash your face in the AM, neck at night.

A SHORT HISTORY OF MEDICINE
"Doctor, I have a bad headache."
2,000 B.C.: "Here, eat this compound of root."
200 A.D.: "Don't touch that root, it is the work of the devil. Say a prayer to God."
1850 A.D.: "Prayer won't help. Take this potion."
1940 A.D.: "That potion is snake oil, just swallow this pill."
1975 A.D.: "That pill is not effective. Here, take this antibiotic."
2010 A.D.: "Antibiotics make germs stronger. Here, eat this compound of root."

I used to feel like a man trapped in a woman's body. But then I was born.

Losing a husband can be hard. In my case, it was almost impossible.

He's such a gentleman; he reminds me of St. Paul, one of the dullest cities in America.
-Henny Youngman

Lottery: a tax on people who don't understand statistics.

Learn from your parents' mistakes. Use birth control.

Stupidity got us into this mess. Why can't it get us out?

Justice is a decision in your favor.

Laughing stock: cattle with a sense of humor.

Bumper sticker: MAKE LOVE, NOT WAR. SEE DRIVER FOR DETAILS.

Meandering to a different drummer.

My wife keeps complaining that I never listen to her ... or something like that.

I'm fat. When I go to a restaurant, they don't give me a menu; they give me an estimate.

I just signed up for group insurance. If I die in a group, I get $100,000.

A man sent 20 different puns to his friends, with the hope that at least 10 of the puns would make them laugh. No pun in 10 did.

Nothing in the known universe travels faster than a bad check.

An optimist is someone who always sees the bright side of your problem.

Make yourself at home! Clean my kitchen.

Old musicians never die. They just decompose.

Politics: poli (many) tics (blood-sucking parasites.)

Rehab is for quitters.

Puritanism: the bothersome idea that someone, somewhere, may be happy.

Some people just don't know how to drive. I call these people 'everybody but me.'

Support your local Search and Rescue. Get lost!

Sex on television can't really hurt you ... unless you fall off.

ALTERED DICTIONARY
Dopeler effect – the tendency of stupid ideas to seem smarter when they come at you rapidly.
Foreploy – any misrepresentation about yourself for the purpose of getting sex.
Giraffiti – vandalism spray-painted very very high.
Glibido – all talk and no action.
Hipatitis – terminal coolness.
Ignoranus – someone both stupid and an asshole.
Inoculatte – to take coffee intravenously.
Intaxication – euphoria at getting a tax refund—which lasts until you realize it's your money to begin with.
Osteopornosis – a degenerate disease.
Reintarnation – coming back to life as a hillbilly.
Sound sleeper – someone who snores.
Squandry – how to spend a sudden windfall very quickly.
Caffeind – someone who really needs coffee.

MORE GREAT HENNY YOUNGMAN CLASSICS

My mother was 88 years old and didn't need glasses. Drank right out of the bottle.

The food on the plane was fit for a king. "Here, King!"

The convict was about to go to the electric chair. He called his lawyer for advice. The lawyer said, "Don't sit down."

A man goes to a psychiatrist, who says, "You're crazy." "I want a second opinion," the man says. "Okay, you're ugly, too."

A panhandler says to me, "Mister, I haven't tasted food for a week."
I say, "Don't worry. It still tastes the same."

My father was never home. He was always away drinking booze. He saw a sign that said "Drink Canada Dry" so he went right up there.

What do you get when you divide the diameter of a pumpkin by its circumference?
Pumpkin Pi

Great One Liners

Why are there fences around cemeteries?
Because people are dying to get in.

Why didn't the skeleton cross the road?
He didn't have the guts.

What did the Mommy ghost say to the baby ghost?
Don't spook until you're spooken to.

What kind of protozoa likes Hallowe'en?
An amoeboo!

How does the witch know what time it is?
She looks at her witch watch.

Veni, Vidi, Visa. I came, I saw, I shopped.

What are the three words no woman wants to hear while she's making love? "Honey, I'm home!"

To err is human. To moo, bovine.

What do you call a lawyer with an IQ of 50?
Your Honor.

In America, anyone can become President. That's the problem.
-George Carlin

YOU KNOW IT'S A BAD DAY WHEN...

Your car horn sticks on the highway behind 32 Hell's Angels bikers.

Your birthday cake collapses under the weight of the candles.

Your 4-year-old tells you that it's almost impossible to flush a grapefruit down the toilet.

You get to work and find a "60 Minutes" team waiting for you.

You turn on the evening news and they're showing emergency routes out of the city.

It costs more to fill up the car than it did to buy it.

Your income tax refund check bounces.

Your blind date turns out to be your ex.

My hope is that soon the gays will be running the world because then there would be no war, just an emphasis on military apparel.

-Roseanne Barr

Capital punishment would be more effective as a preventive measure if it were administered prior to the crime.

-Woody Allen

The cure for boredom is curiosity. There is no cure for curiosity.

-Dorothy Parker

If a man watches three football games in a row, he should be declared legally dead.

-Erma Bombeck

A woman came up to me on the street and said, "You know, a cow was murdered to make your suede jacket!" I replied: "I didn't know there were any witnesses. Now I'll have to kill you, too."

-Jake Johansen

MORE OF THE TWISTED DICTIONARY

Babysitter: a small child who has not yet learned how to walk or crawl.

Bernadette: the act of torching the mortgage.

Cookout: the cook's day off.

Cowhide: Hide and Seek played by cattle.

Dog paddle: a rolled newspaper to punish the dog without hurting him.

Fan club: weapon used by a celebrity to beat off too many fans.

Flying saucers: the wife is on a rampage.

Girl scout: a boy who hunts for girls.

Hardship: a boat protected with a heavy covering.

Headlight: a dizzy spell.

High school: a school atop the Sears Tower.

Hence: an enclosure for hens.

Holy smoke: a church on fire.

Polarize: what penguins see with.

Body by Fischer ... Brains by Mattel

The little boy said to his annoyed mother, "But Mommy the dog only cost five cents and it's going to have puppies!"

I just broke up with someone and the last thing she said to me was, "You'll never find anyone like me again!" I'm thinking, I should hope not!

I had a linguistics professor who said that it's man's ability to use language that makes him the dominant species. That may be. But I think there's one other thing that separates us from animals. We aren't afraid of the vacuum cleaner.
    -Jeff Stilson

I've been doing the Fonda workout. The Peter Fonda workout. That's where I wake up, take a hit of acid, smoke a joint, and go to my sister's house and ask for money.
    -Kevin Meany

A woman broke up with me and sent me pictures of her in bed with her new boyfriend. My revenge? I sent them on to her Dad.
    -Christopher Case

I had a rose named after me and was very flattered. But I was not pleased to read the description in the catalog: No good in a bed, but fine against a wall.
-Eleanor Roosevelt

Be careful about reading health books. You may die of a misprint.
-Mark Twain

I got off the train at Grand Central Station. I was so happy. I looked up at the beautiful ceiling and cried, "New York, New York!" Then I looked down, and my luggage was gone; and I knew I really <u>was</u> in New York, New York!

My wife has a slight impediment in her speech. Every now and then she stops to breathe.
-Jimmy Durante

My luck is so bad that if I bought a cemetery, people would stop dying.
-Rodney Dangerfield

We have found that William Tell and his family were all avid bowlers. However, all the Swiss league records were destroyed in a fire, and we'll never know for whom the Tells bowled.

Women complain about premenstrual syndrome, but I think of it as the only time of the month that I can be myself.
-Roseanne Barr

Actually, it only takes one drink to get me loaded. Trouble is, I can't remember if it's the thirteenth or the fourteenth.
-George Burns

One perfect child, and every Mom has it.

A child's greatest period of growth is the month after you've purchased new school uniforms.

My wife and I always compromise. I admit I'm wrong and she agrees with me.

You're getting old when you enjoy remembering things more than doing them.

Laziness is nothing more than the habit of resting before you get tired.

Power corrupts; but we need the electricity.

A Mormon threw out his mothers-in-law and emptied Salt Lake City.

Bad officials are elected by good citizens who don't vote.

Those who can't laugh at themselves leave the job to others.

Real friends are those who survive transitions between address books.

Marriage is a relationship where one person is always right and the other is the husband.

They call our language the mother tongue because the father so seldom gets to speak.

Why do couples hold hands during the marriage ceremony? It's a formality, just like two boxers shaking hands before the fight begins.

When told she needed a visa for China, the woman exclaimed: "I've been to China four times and they always accepted my Amex card!"

In this economy, you have to choose between tightening your belt or losing your pants.

You may have a heart of gold, but so does a hard-boiled egg.

If Hamlet took place in the U.S., would he be arrested for Polonius assault?

What's a blonde's idea of natural childbirth? She's not wearing makeup.

Everyone should get married. After all, happiness is not the only thing in life.

Our marriage was a love match, plain and simple. She was plain and I was simple.

IT'S A BAD DAY WHEN...
...you have to sit down to brush your teeth in the morning.
...you need one bathroom scale for each foot.
...you wake up and your braces are stuck together.
...the bird singing outside your window is a vulture.
...your car payment, house payment and girlfriend are all three months overdue.
...you begin to hang up the clothes you wore home from the party--and there aren't any.
...you realize that the phone number on the bathroom wall of the bar is yours.

Black holes: where God divided by zero.

All power corrupts, but we need the electricity.

MORE GEORGE BURNS CLASSICS:
When I was a boy, the Dead Sea was only sick.

Too bad that all the people who know how to run the country are busy driving taxicabs and cutting hair.

Look to the future because that's where you'll be spending the rest of your life.

If it's a good script, I'll do it. And if it's a bad script and they pay me enough, I'll do it.

I smoke 10 to 15 cigars a day. At my age, I have to hold on to something.

I don't believe in dying. It's been done. I'm looking for a new exit. Besides, I can't die now—I'm booked. I can't afford to die; I'd lose too much money.

Traffic signals in New York City are just rough guidelines.
-David Letterman

Democracy means that anyone can grow up to be President, and anyone who doesn't grow up can be Vice-President.
-Johnny Carson

If you don't disagree with me, how will I know I'm right?
-Samuel Goldwyn

I spent most of my money on booze and women. The rest I wasted.

Nowadays, every Tom Dick and Harry is named Michael.

How come the dove gets to be the peace symbol? How about the pillow? It has more feathers than the dove and it doesn't have that sharp beak.

One time, a guy pulled a knife on me. I could tell it wasn't a professional job; it had butter on it.
-Rodney Dangerfield

A long dispute means both parties are wrong.

A lost ounce of gold may be found, a lost moment of time—never.

A long life may not be good enough, but a good life is long enough.
-Benjamin Franklin

There is certainly more in the future now than back in 1964.
-Roger Daltrey

Researchers have discovered that chocolate produces some of the same reactions in the brain as marijuana. They also discovered other similarities, but can't remember what they are.
-Matt Lauer

I love California. I practically grew up in Phoenix.
-Dan Quayle

We apologize for the error in last week's paper in which we said that Mr. Arnold Dogbody was a defective in the police force. We meant, of course, that he is a detective in the police farce.

We're overpaying him, but he's worth it.
-Samuel Goldwyn

I saw that show, '50 Things to Do Before You Die.' I would have thought the obvious one was: "Shout for help!"
-Mark Watson

Employee of the month is a good example of how somebody can be both a winner and a loser at the same time.

-Demitri Martin

A dog goes into a hardware store and says, "I'd like a job." The owner says, "We don't hire dogs. Why don't you join a circus?" The dog answers: "What would the circus want with a plumber?"

-Steven Alan Green

I love deadlines. I especially love the whooshing sound they make as they fly by.

-Douglas Adams

Cats have nine lives. Which makes them ideal for experimentation.

-Jimmy Carr

I've been to Canada and I've always gotten the impression that I could take the country over in two days.

-Jon Stewart

Save the whales. Trade them for valuable prizes!

Half this game is ninety percent mental.

-Danny Ozark, Phillies manager

Can you imagine what would have happened if Columbus had a wife. All he had to do was tell her that Queen Isabella gave him 3 ships for nothing!

The lottery is a tax on idiots. Or on people who can't do math.

Smoking kills, and if you're killed, you've lost a very important part of your life.
    -Brooke Shields

China is a big country, inhabited by many Chinese.
    -Charles de Gaulle

Oscar is 80 this year, which makes him now automatically the frontrunner for the Republican nomination.
    -Jon Stewart

I can't understand how I flunked American history. When I was a kid there was so little of it.
    -George Burns

All sun all the time creates a desert.

What are two reasons men don't mind their own business?
    1. No mind.   2. No business

What did God say after creating Man? I can do better.

What's the different between a porcupine and a Porsche?
The porcupine has pricks on the outside.

The second day of a diet is always easier than the first. By the second day, you're off it.
-Jackie Gleason

The reason most people play golf is to wear clothes they would not be caught dead in otherwise.

Anytime four New Yorkers get into a cab together without arguing, a bank robbery has just taken place.
-Johnny Carson

A cement mixer collided with a prison van on the Kingston Pass. Motorists are asked to be on the lookout for sixteen hardened criminals.
-Ronnie Corbett

I souport publik edekasion.

The trouble with history is that every time it repeats itself, the prices go up.

Back up my hard drive? How do I put it in reverse?

You have the right to remain silent. Anything you say will be misquoted and then used against you.

I like you, but I wouldn't want to see you working with subatomic particles.

He's not dead. He's only electroencephalographically challenged.

Men reach their sexual peak at 18. Women reach theirs at 35. Do you get the feeling that God is playing a practical joke?
-Rita Rudner

There's a helluva distance between wisecracking and wit. Wit has truth in it; wisecracking is simply calisthenics with words.
-Dorothy Parker

One thing they never tell you about child raising is that for the rest of your life, at the drop of a hat, you are expected to know your child's name and how old he or she is.
-Erma Bombeck

My husband and I are either going to buy a dog or have a child. We can't decide whether to ruin our carpet or our lives.

-Rita Rudner

I celebrated Thanksgiving just like the original one. I invited everyone in my neighborhood to my house, we had an enormous feast and then I killed them and took their land.

-Jon Stewart

I have a daughter who goes to SMU. She could've gone to UCLA, but it's one more letter she'd have to remember.

-Shecky Greene

A conference is a gathering of important people who, singly, can do nothing; but get together and decide that nothing can be done.

-Fred Allen

I miss my wife's cooking ... as often as possible.

-Henny Youngman

If law school is so hard to get through, how come there are so many lawyers?

-Calvin Trillin

Don't spend two dollars to have a shirt laundered. Donate it to the Salvation Army instead. They'll clean it and put it on a hanger and next morning you can buy it back for 75 cents.
-William Coronel

I was going to have plastic surgery until I noticed that the doctor's office was full of portraits by Picasso.
-Rita Rudner

MORE FROM THE TWISTED DICTIONARY:
Arcade – a kind of lemonade served on Noah's ark.
Band-Aid – a fund to help a band.
Contents – where con men sleep on a camping trip.
Detail – removing a tail.
Eyedropper – a clumsy optometrist.
Funny paper – paper that laughs.
Ghost town – a town full of haunted houses.
Goodbye – a bargain.
Hatchet – what a hen does to an egg.
Heavy duty – loading an elephant.
Himalaya – a rooster that lays an egg.
Ideal – a person who wants to deal every time.
Layaway Plan – a pre-arranged burial plan.
Little Dipper – a small child diving.
Monkey business – a store run by monkeys.
Polite – a light on a pole.
Priesthood – special headgear for a priest.

Protest – testing a professional person.
Rest Stop – the traffic light is stuck on red.
Single entry – only unmarried people allowed in.
Yearbook – a book that takes a year to read.

The only "ism" Hollywood believes in is plagarism.
-Dorothy Parker

He would drink a nip in the air.

How is a man like a snowstorm?
You don't know when it's coming, how many inches you'll get, and how long it'll stay.

If history repeats itself, I should think we can expect the same thing again.
-Terry Venables

"It is beyond my apprehension."
-baseball team manager

"I want something for fleas."
"Get a dog."

"This is unparalyzed in the state's history."
-Gib Lewis, Texas Speaker of the House

The more I think of you the less I think of you.
-Henny Youngman

"Sure, there have been injuries and deaths in boxing – but none of them serious."
-anonymous

I saw a woman wearing a tshirt that said "Guess?"
"Thyroid problem?" I asked.

You're trapped in a room with a tiger, a snake and a lawyer. Your gun has two bullets. What do you do?
Shoot the lawyer twice.

If a long dress is evening wear, what is a suit of armor? Silverware.

What can you hold without ever touching it?
A conversation.

What do you get when you cross poison ivy with a 4-leaf clover? A rash of good luck.

What do you get when you cross an insect with the Easter rabbit? Bugs Bunny

What do you get when you cross a stream and a brook? Wet feet.

Henry Ford, despite his great wealth, never owned a Cadillac.

Why do blondes write TGIF on their shoes? Toes Go In Front.

Why did the blonde tiptoe past the medicine cabinet? She didn't want to wake the sleeping pills.

Because your bride has been given away, don't imagine that she'll be cheap.

Never play peekaboo with a child on a long plane trip. There's no end to the game. Finally I grabbed him by the bib and said, "Look, it's always gonna be me!"
-Rita Rudner

The art of never making a mistake is crucial to motherhood. A mother must have her children believe she has never engaged in sex, never made a bad decision, never caused her own mother a moment's anxiety, and was never a child.
-Erma Bombeck

7/5th of all people do not understand fractions.

Prices are just too high these days, I asked the deli man for two dollars' worth of Swiss cheese. He wrapped up six holes.

A bird does not sing because it has an answer; it sings because it has a song.

Holy smoke: a church on fire.

A wide screen just makes a bad movie twice as bad.
-Samuel Goldwyn

A wedding is a funeral where you can smell your own flowers.

Disney has the best casting. If he doesn't like an actor, he just tears him up.
-Alfred Hitchcock

SIR WINSTON CHURCHILL CLASSICS
A cat will look down to a man. A dog will look up to a man. But a pig will look you straight in the eye and see his equal.

A fanatic is one who can't change his mind and won't change the subject.

Although prepared for martyrdom, I preferred that it be postponed.

A lie gets halfway around the world before the truth has a chance to get its pants on.

A pessimist sees the difficulty in every opportunity. An optimist sees the opportunity in every difficulty.

Ending a sentence with a preposition is something up with which I will not put.

History will be kind to me for I intend to write it.

I am ready to meet my Maker. Whether my Maker is prepared for the great ordeal of meeting me is another matter.

He has all the virtues I dislike and none of the vices I admire.

If you are going through Hell, keep going.

It has been said that democracy is the worst form of government...except for all the others.

Statistics are like a drunk with a lamp post... used more for support than illumination.

The greatest lesson in life is to know that even fools are right sometimes.

Success is the ability to go from one failure to another without a loss of enthusiasm.

Most jocks have an intellect rivaled only by garden tools.

Drama is life with the dull bits cut out.

PEOPLE WHO WORK IN THE MOVIES

Every time an Oscar is given out, an agent gets his wings.
-Kathy Bates

Film is one of the three universal languages, the other two being math and music.
-Frank Capra

I did a picture in England one winter and it was so cold, I almost got married.
-Shelley Winters

Go see that turkey for yourself, and see for yourself why you shouldn't see it.
-Samuel Goldwyn

Film is the art of illiterates.
-Werner Herzog

Goodbye, Mr. Zanuck, it certainly has been a pleasure working for Sixteenth Century Fox.
-Jean Renoir

I shouldn't make movies. I should go to a lunatic asylum.
-Werner Herzog

I steal from every movie ever made.
-Quentin Tarantino

I always think that sex looks kind of funny in a movie.
-Wm. Friedkin

I'd have thrashed him to within an inch of his life, but I didn't have a tape measure with me.
-Groucho Marx

I thought "Deep Throat" was a movie about a giraffe.
-Bob Hope

The camera lies 24 times per second.
-Brian de Palma

I've been close to Bette Davis for 38 years—and I have the cigarette burns to prove it.
-Henry Fonda

I've made so many movies playing a hooker that they don't pay me in the regular way any more. They leave it on the dresser.
-Shirley MacLaine

If my films make one more person miserable, I'll feel I have done my job.
-Woody Allen

In feature films, the director is God; in documentary films God is the director.
-Alfred Hitchcock

If I were in this business only for the business, I wouldn't be in this business.
-Samuel Goldwyn

I've got a good mind to join a club and beat you over the head with it.
-Groucho Marx

The trouble with Bogart is, he thinks he's Bogart.
-John Houston

They used to shoot Shirley Temple through gauze. They should shoot me through linoleum.
-Tallulah Bankhead

So where's the Cannes Film Festival being held this year?
-Christina Aguilera

Shirley Temple had charisma as a child; but it cleared up as an adult.
-Totie Fields

Violence is one of the most fun things to watch.
-Quentin Tarantino

Why is it a garage door opener when it both opens and closes the garage door.

RED BUTTONS CLASSICS

Ben Hur said to his sister Ben Him, "We'd better swap names before they start calling me Ben Gay!"

George Washington said to his father: "Dad, if I never tell a lie, how am I ever gonna be President?"

Abraham Lincoln said: "A house divided... is a condominium."

Nero's wife Shirley said to him: "Idiot! Fiddle on the *roof!* You'll make a fortune!"

James Cagney said to Mickey Mouse: "You dirty rat!"

Moshe Dayan donated his eye to CBS.

Adam said to Eve, "What do you mean, you got nothing to wear?"

Eve said to Adam: "Does this fig leaf make me look fat?"

King Henry VIII said to his lawyer, "Forget the alimony. I've got a better idea."

Venus de Milo's mother said: "You never call me. Can't you pick up a phone?"

Noah's wife said to him, after 40 days and 40 nights, "It's *your* turn to spread papers on the floor."

King Solomon said to his thousand wives: "Who doesn't have a headache tonight?"

Sleeping Beauty to the Prince: "Are you sure all we did was kiss?"

HENNY YOUNGMAN FAVORITES

If you had your life to live over again, do it overseas.

My brother was a lifeguard in a car wash.

When God sneezed, I didn't know what to say.

I've got all the money I'll ever need ... if I die by four o'clock.

I told the doctor I broke my leg in two places. He told me to stop going to those places.

The horse I bet on was so slow, the jockey kept a diary.

The man used to go to school with his dog and then they were separated. The dog graduated!

Did you hear about the optician? Two glasses and he made a spectacle of himself.

I haven't taken my Christmas lights down yet. They look so nice on the pumpkin.
-Winston Spear

Every time a baseball player grabs his crotch, it makes him spit. That's why you should never date a baseball player.
-Marsha Warfield

Snowboarding is an activity very popular with people who do not feel that skiing is lethal enough.
-Dave Barry

The ad in the paper said Big Sale. Last Week. Why advertise? I already missed it. They're just rubbing it in.
-Yacov Smirnoff

Everything that used to be a sin is now a disease.
-Bill Maher

Subdued: a guy on a submarine.

You make the beds, you do the dishes—and six months later, you have to start all over again
-Joan Rivers

That married couples can live together day after day after day is a miracle the Vatican has overlooked.
-Bill Cosby

"Doctor, I can't stop singing "The Green, Green Grass of Home."

"That sounds like Tom Jones Syndrome."

"Is it common?"

"It's not unusual."

When the sun comes up, I have morals again.
-Elayne Boosler

Our comedies are not to be laughed at.
-Samuel Goldwyn

Success is never final.
-Sir Winston Churchill

When Ginger Rogers danced with Astaire, it was the only time in movies when you looked at the man, not the woman.
-Gene Kelly

A good film is when the price of the dinner, the theater admission, and the babysitter are all worth it.
-Alfred Hitchcock

I thought Star Wars was too wacky for the general public.
-George Lucas

Hollywood is a place where they'll pay you a thousand dollars for a kiss and 50 cents for your soul.
-Marilyn Monroe

Everyone has his day and some days last longer than others.
-Sir Winston Churchill

You know what your problem is? It's that you haven't seen enough movies. All of life's riddles are answered in the movies.
-Steve Martin

Progress is made by lazy men looking for an easier way to do things.

What does a spy do when he gets cold? He goes undercover.

The Miss Universe pageant is fixed. All the winners are always from Earth.

We are all time travelers, moving at the speed of exactly 60 minutes per hour.

Vegetarian: native American definition of a lousy hunter.

I read recipes the same way I read scienc
I get to the end and I think, "Well, that's not goi ⌣ ⌄
happen."

The difference between fiction and reality? Fiction
has to make sense.

Alcohol is a perfect solvent: it dissolves marriages,
families, and careers.

Children seldom misquote you. In fact, they
usually repeat word for word what you shouldn't
have said.

George Washington said that we would have a
black president "when pigs fly." Well, swine flu.

I have never understood why women love cats.
Cats are independent, they don't listen, they don't come
in when you call them, they like to stay out all night, and
when they're home they like to be left alone to sleep. In
other words, every quality that women hate in a man,
they love in a cat.

Brought up to respect the conventions, love had to
end in marriage. And I'm afraid it did.
     -Bette Davis

Gravitation cannot be blamed for people falling in love.
-Albert Einstein

If love is the answer, could you please rephrase the question?
-Lily Tomlin

Life is pain and the enjoyment of love is an anesthetic.

Love is the most difficult and dangerous form of courage.
-Delmore Schwartz

Love is friendship set on fire.

The perfect lover is one who turns into a pizza at 4:00 AM

If you can't convince them, confuse them.

Why do people keep running over a string a dozen times with their vacuum cleaner, then reach down, pick it up, examine it, then put it back down to give their vacuum one more chance?

The big difference between sex for money and sex for love is that sex for money usually costs a lot less.

Love is the delightful interval between meeting a beautiful girl and discovering that she looks like a haddock.
-John Barrymore

He has the gift of compressing the largest amount of words into the smallest amount of thoughts.
-Sir Winston Churchill

Those two are a fastidious couple. She's fast and he's hideous.

Women are like elephants. I like to watch them but I wouldn't want to own one.
-W.C. Fields

When the Academy called, I panicked. I thought they might want their Oscars back and the pawn shop has been out of business for awhile.
-Woody Allen

Why should people go out and pay to see bad movies when they can stay home and watch bad television?
-Samuel Goldwyn

Refuse: to replace a burnt-out fuse.

By the time a man realizes his father was right, he has a son who thinks he's wrong.

Does time fly when you're having sex, or was it really just two minutes?

Why didn't Noah swat those two mosquitoes?

We've all heard that a million monkeys banging on a million typewriters will eventually reproduce the entire works of Shakespeare. Now, thanks to the internet, we know this isn't true.

It's amazing that the amount of news happening in the world every day always just exactly fits the newspaper.

According to a new survey, women say they feel more comfortable undressing in front of men than they do undressing in front of other women. Women are too judgmental where, of course, men are just grateful.

Well, aren't you a waste of 2 billion years of evolution!

The right to be heard does not automatically include the right to be taken seriously.

If you're looking for sympathy, you'll find it in the dictionary between "shit" and "syphilis."

Two years ago, I married a lovely young virgin, and if that doesn't change pretty soon, I'm gonna get a divorce.

To err is human, to blame it on somebody else shows managerial potential.

I'm a humble person, really. I'm actually much greater than I think I am.

America is a country that produces citizens who will cross the ocean to fight for democracy but won't cross the street to vote.

The hardest thing in life to learn is which bridge to burn and which to cross.

Don't steal. That's the government's job.

I'm multi-talented. I can talk and piss you off at the same time.

My drinking team has a bowling problem.

People tend to make rules for others and exceptions for themselves.

Drink coffee! Do stupid things faster, with more energy!

A celebrity is someone who works very hard all his life to become known and then wears dark glasses to avoid being recognized.

Sometimes the best helping hand you can give is a good firm push.

The easiest job in the world has to be coroner. Surgery on dead people. What's the worst thing that could happen? If something went wrong, maybe you'd get a pulse.

One in five people in the world are Chinese. There are 5 people in my family, so it must be one of them. It's either my Mom or my Dad. Or my older brother Colin. Or my younger brother Ho Cha Chin. But I think it's Colin.

Lite: the new way to spell "light," now with 20% fewer letters.

Why don't you slip into something more comfortable ... like a coma.

A positive attitude may not solve all your problems, but it will annoy enough people to make it worth the effort.

If Wal-Mart is lowering the prices every day, why isn't everything in the store free yet?

Alcoholism is the only disease that tries to convince you that you don't have it.

I sometimes go to my own little world. But that's okay; they know me there.

During sex, my girlfriend always wants to talk to me. Just the other night she called me from a hotel.

They keep saying the right person will come along. I think mine got hit by a truck.

A committee is a group doing the work of one.

We are all part of the ultimate statistic. Ten out of ten people die.

If you must choose between two evils, pick the one you've never done before.

When we were together, you always said you would die for me. Now that we broke up, I think it's time you kept your word.

Just about the time you think you can make ends meet, somebody moves the ends.

It's not how good your work it, it's how well you explain it.

Every so often, I like to go to the window, look up, and smile for a satellite picture.

You can easily judge the character of a man by how he treats those who can do nothing for him.

Some of us learn from the mistakes of others. The rest of us have to be the others.

I wondered why people seem to read the Bible a whole lot more as they get older. Then it dawned on me. They're cramming for their finals.

At every party, there are two kinds of people: those who want to go home and those who don't. The trouble is, they're usually married to each other.

Silence doesn't mean your sexual performance left her speechless.

Canadians are more polite when they're being rude than Americans are when they're being friendly.

I said "no" to drugs, but they wouldn't listen.

If you do not say it, they cannot repeat it.

Failure is not falling down; it's not getting up again.

If a leper gives you the finger, do you have to give it back?

The best thing about living at the beach is that you only have idiots on three sides of you.

The human brain is a wonderful thing. It starts working the moment you're born and doesn't stop until you stand up to speak in public.

Why do women always ask questions that have no right answers?

Insanity is defined as doing the same thing over and over, expecting different results.

Trust, but verify.

Men are like mascara. They usually run at the first sign of emotion.

Sometimes when I reflect back on all the beer I drink I feel ashamed... then I look into the glass and think about the workers in the brewery and all of their hopes and dreams. If I don't drink this beer, they might be out of work and those dreams would be shattered. Then I say to myself, "It is better that I drink this beer and let their dreams come true than be selfish and worry about my liver."

I ran three miles today. Finally, I said, "Okay, lady, take back your purse."

The main difference between the men I've dated and Charles Manson is that Manson has the decency to look like a nut case when you first meet him.

Life's a bitch, because if it was a slut, it'd be easy.

When you go to the drugstore, why aren't the condoms in with all the other party supplies?

Laugh and the world laughs with you. Snore and you sleep alone.

There are two kinds of people who don't say much: those who are quiet and those who talk a lot.

Accept it: your parents HAVE had sex.

When you stop believing in Santa Claus is when you start getting clothes for Christmas.

It's not the bullet that kills you; it's the hole.

Friends are like condoms. They protect you when things get hard.

Being in a nudist colony probably takes all the fun out of Halloween.

A cheap shot is a terrible thing to waste.

The best contraception for old folks is nudity.

Have you been to Wal-Mart lately? You have to weight 300 pounds to get the automatic doors to open.

born to be a pessimist. My blood type is B

I used to be a lifeguard, but some blue kid got me fired.

Follow your dreams, except for the ones where you're naked at work.

I had amnesia once … maybe twice.

Which one of these is the non-smoking lifeboat?

I've been on so many blind dates, I should get a free dog.

There is no "I" in "team," but there are four in "platitude-quoting idiot."

If at first you don't succeed, try left field.

It's not who you know, it's whom you know.

Marriage isn't a word; it's a sentence.

Treat each day as your last because one day you'll be right.

Great One Liners

Contents may have settled out of court.

There are two rules for success. 1) don't tell all you know.

I like my men the way I like my coffee: ground up and in the freezer.

I like my women the way I like my coffee: cold and bitter.

A fool and his money can throw one helluva party.

Photons have mass? I didn't even know they were Catholic.

If I agreed with you, we'd both be wrong.

Men have two emotions: hungry and horny. If you see him without an erection, make him a sandwich.

We never really grow up; we only learn how to behave in public.

The voices in my head may not be real, but they have some pretty good ideas.

Whenever I fill out an application, in the part that says, "If an emergency, notify..." I put "DOCTOR." What's my mother going to do?

Cremation? Think outside the box.

I don't trust anything that bleeds for five days and doesn't die.

You're never too old to learn something stupid.

To be sure of hitting the target, shoot first and call what you hit the target.

With sufficient thrust, pigs fly just fine.

Worrying works. 90% of the things I worry about never happen.

You're such a good friend that if we were on a sinking ship with only one lifejacket left ... I'd miss you terribly and think of you every day!

The trouble with doing something right the first time is that nobody appreciates how difficult it was.

How do you draw a blank?

Could crop circles be the work of a cereal killer?

How do I set my laser printer on stun?

How can something be "new and improved?" If it's new, what's it improving on?

What the world really needs is more love and less paperwork.
-Pearl Bailey

Everybody is somebody's weirdo.

How do "DON'T WALK ON GRASS" signs get there?

My wife dresses to kill. She cooks the same way.

The length of a film should be directly related to the endurance of the human bladder.
-Alfred Hitchcock

I like you. You remind me of when I was young and stupid.

He may look like an idiot and talk like an idiot, but don't let that fool you. He really is an idiot.
-Groucho Marx

I like your approach. Now let me see your departure.

I don't know what your problem is, but I'll bet it's hard to pronounce.

A sharp tongue does not mean you have a keen mind.

He doesn't know the meaning of fear ... but then again, he doesn't know the meaning of <u>most</u> words.

Did Noah keep his bees in archives?

He is so short, that when it's raining, he's always the last to know.

I'd like to give you a going-away present. But first, do <u>your</u> part.

His personality is split so many ways, he goes for group therapy on his own.

Make somebody happy. Mind your own business.

How come we say "tunafish" but not "beefmammal" or "chickenbird?"

If cocaine were legal, would they sell it in little packets like Sweet'n'Low? They could call it Sweet'N'High.

Is it possible for someone to become addicted to therapy? If so, how could we treat them?

I'm busy. Can I ignore you another time?

You're not as bad as people say. You're much much worse.

You are validating my inherent distrust of strangers.

I'm retired. I was tired yesterday and I'm tired again today.

It might look like I'm doing nothing; but at the cellular level, I'm really quite busy.

Thank you. We're all refreshed and challenged by your unique point of view.

How can there be self-help groups?

Yes, I am an agent of Satan; but my duties are largely ceremonial.

You sound reasonable. I think it's time to up my medication.

I don't remember being absent-minded.

I'm out of my mind, but feel free to leave a message.

There are a terrible lot of lies going around the world, and the worst of it is, half of them are true.
-Sir Winston Churchill

It is better to be feared than loved, if you cannot be both.
-Machiavelli

Nothing takes the taste out of peanut butter like unrequited love.
-Charlie Brown (Charles Schultz)

A penny saved is a Congressional spending oversight.

My mind works like lightning: one brilliant flash and it's gone.

It's easier to get older than to get wiser.

When I'm finally holding all the cards, why does everyone decide to play chess?

Even crime wouldn't pay if the government ran it.

If God wanted me to touch my toes, he would have put them on my knees.

I started out with zero a still have most of it.

I finally got my head together and now my body is falling apart.

My mind makes contracts my body can't keep.

I regret making all those mistakes resisting temptation.

These days, an "all nighter" means I didn't have to get up to pee.

Now that I know all the answers, nobody asks e any questions.

The definition of a queer Irishman: one who prefers women to drink.

I must be getting old. My back goes out more than I do.

I must be getting old. I can live without sex but not without my glasses.

I must be getting old. I can throw a party and the neighbors don't even realize it.

Marriage is a good way for a woman to keep active until the right man comes along.

I feel like the morning after—and I haven't been anywhere!

My favorite mythical creature? The honest politician.

They accuse me of being crude—that's bullshit!
-Mel Brooks

I refuse to have a battle of wits with an unarmed person.

Love is like the measles; we all have to go through it.
-Jerome K. Jerome

Sometimes I lie awake at night, and I ask, "Where have I gone wrong?" Then a voice says to me, "This is going to take more than one night."
-Charles Schulz

Lefties are among the first to demand rights.

Thousands have lived without love, not one without water.
-W. H. Auden

Many a man has fallen in love with a girl in a light so dim he would not have chosen a suit by it.
-Maurice Chevalier

If someone leads but no one follows ... is he just out for a walk?

Why do they have handicapped parking in front of a gym?

I must be getting older. Half the stuff in my shopping cart says, "for fast relief."

I must be getting older. 6:00 AM is when I get up, not when I go to bed.

I must be getting old. Getting a little action means I don't have to take a laxative.

My son complains about headaches. I keep telling him: when you get out of bed, <u>feet first!</u>

I will defend, to your death, my right to my own opinions.

I'm blonde. What's your excuse?

I asked my wife what old men wear: briefs or boxers? She said Depends.

Who am I calling stupid? Good question. What's your name?

You're not yourself today. I noticed the improvement immediately.

If the good die young, what does that say about senior citizens?

I'm not old. I'm chronologically gifted.

How do you know when it's time to tune your bagpipes?

Needing a man is like needing a parachute. If he isn't there the first time you need him, chances are you won't be needing him again.

I can please only one person per day. Today is not your day. Tomorrow isn't looking good either.

I'm as broke as the 10 Commandments.

Good news is just life's way of keeping you off balance.

Someday we'll look back on all this and plow into a parked car.

God did not create the world in seven days; he messed around for six days and then pulled an all-nighter.

If stupidity was music, you'd be a band.

The best things in life are free ... or at least have no interest or payments for one full year.

My parents were so poor, they got married for the rice.

Men are like bank accounts. Without money, they don't generate much interest.

Money can't buy everything ... but then again, neither can no money.

FROM THE FERTILE MIND OF STEVEN WRIGHT

It's a small world, but I wouldn't want to have to paint it.

My watch is three hours fast, and I can't fix it. So I'm going to move to New York.

He asked me if I knew what time it was. I said, "Yes, but not right now."

I got a new shadow. I had to get rid of the other one; it wasn't doing what I was doing.

Right now, I'm having amnesia and deja-vu at the same time. I think I've forgotten this before.

I'm moving to Mars next week, so if you have any boxes...

I talk to myself a lot and it bothers other people because I like to use a megaphone.

Great One Liners

I like to leave messages before the beep.

I bought some powdered water but don't know what to add.

You know when you're sitting in a chair and you lean back so you're on just two legs and you almost fall over and at the last second you catch yourself? I feel like that all the time.

I have a telescope on the peep hole of my door so I can see who is at the door for 200 miles.

Not afraid of heights; afraid of widths.

Mommy is the name of God on children's lips.

You should never say anything to a woman that even remotely suggests that you think she's pregnant, unless you can see an actual baby emerging from her at that moment.
   -Dave Barry

Would you like some cheese and crackers to go with that whine?

They have a big problem at nudist weddings. Where do you keep the ring?

I got up the other day and everything in my apartment had been stolen and replaced with exact replicas.

MURPHY'S LAW ON WORK

If at first you don't succeed, try again. Then quit. No use being a fool about it.

Mother said there would be days like this, but she didn't say there would be so many.

Everything can be filed under "miscellaneous."

The more crap you put up with, the more crap you are going to get.

A pat on the back is only a few centimeters from a kick in the pants.

Eat one live toad first thing in the morning and nothing worse will happen to you for the rest of the day.

I was just in London. There's a 6 hour time difference. I'm still confused. When I go to dinner, I feel sexy; when I go to bed, I'm hungry.

If the shoe fits ... buy them in every color.

The doctor gave a man six months to live. The man couldn't pay his bill, so the doctor gave him another six months.

Take life with a pinch of salt ... a wedge of lime and a shot of tequila.

In the Jewish tradition, the fetus is not considered viable until it has graduated from medical school.

She loves nature, in spite of what it did to her.

The nice thing about being senile is you can hide your own Easter eggs.

I've sure gotten old! Had two bypasses, a hip replacement, new knees. I'm half blind, half deaf and take 20 different medications that make me dizzy and subject to blackouts. Can hardly feel my hands or feet anymore and can't remember if I'm 89 or 98. I've lost all my friends, but thank God, I still have my driver's license!

Here's how to prevent sagging. Just eat until all the wrinkles fill out.

Diet: penalty for exceeding the feed limit.

It's scary when you start to make the same noises as your coffee maker.

I used to be a proofreader for a skywriting company.

I broke a mirror and am supposed to get 7 years bad luck; but my lawyer thinks he can get me 5.

I lost a button hole.

There's a museum that has all the heads and arms from the statues in the other museums.

Had trouble getting home the other day because I parked in a towaway zone; and when I got back the entire area was gone.

Every morning is the dawn of a new error.

Why are they called "stands" when they're made for sitting?

I'm always slightly terrified when I exit out of my word processor and it asks me if I want to save my changes to a document I swear I didn't make any changes to.

Bad decisions make good stories.

I find it hard to believe that there are actually people who get in the shower first and THEN turn on the water.

A bigamist is a man who makes the same mistake twice at the same time.

The letters T and G are very close to each other on a keyboard... consequently, I will never be ending a work email with the words "regards" again.

I have a hard time distinguishing between boredom and hunger.

My wife is an old-fashioned cook. Why, she's still making radio dinners!

Why did the blonde get fired from the banana plantation? Because she threw out the bent ones.

How come "slow down" and "slow up" mean the same thing?

Everywhere is in walking distance, if you have the time.

I decided to take an aerobics class. I bent, twisted, gyrated, jumped up and down, and perspired for half an hour. But by the time I got my tights on, the class was over.

I used to work in a factory that made fire hydrants, but you couldn't park anywhere near the place.

I have a map of the U.S. that's actual size. It says 1 mile = 1 mile.

I walked up to a girl in a bar and said, "Do you live around here often?"

I told my girlfriend that I was going to die because my birth certificate had an expiration date.

HE: Whatever happened to our sexual relations?
SHE: I don't know. I don't think we even got a Christmas card from them this year.

By the time a man is wise enough to watch his step, he's too old to go anywhere.

Medicine is a great profession. You get a woman to take off her clothes and then you send her husband the bill.

Remember, ladies, wherever there is a good looking, sweet, generous man, there is some woman tired of his bullshit.

When life gets you down, just put on your big girl panties and deal with it!

Middle age is when you still believe you'll feel better in the morning.

Al Jolson's funeral was widely attended by those who wanted to make sure.
-George Jessel

Short summary of every Jewish holiday: They tried to destroy us. We won. Let's eat.

The last person to get across Boston in under three hours was yelling, "The British are coming! The British are coming!"

Doctor: Mr. Smith, your check came back.
Patient: So did my arthritis.

I will always cherish the initial misconceptions I had about you.

The fact that no one understands you doesn't mean you're an artist.

Respectable people do not write music or make love as a career.
-Alexander Borodin

Love is like playing checkers. You have to know which man to move.
-Moms Mabley

You know you're getting older when a $4 bottle of wine is "pretty good stuff."

You know you're getting older, when all you want for your birthday is not to be reminded of your age.

You know you're getting older when everything hurts; and what doesn't hurt, doesn't work.

When I die, I'm leaving my body to science fiction.
-Stephen Wright

Great One-Liners

This is an excellent time to become a missing person.

From the moment I picked up your book until I put it down, I was convulsed with laughter. One of these days, I intend to read it.

When I look into your eyes, I see straight to the back of your head.

You really are as pretty as a picture. I'd love to hang you.

If what you don't know can't hurt you, she's practically invulnerable.

Love comes quietly, without banners or flashing lights. If you hear bells, get your ears checked.
   -Erich Segal

HE: So ... what's your sign?
SHE: Dollar.

I don't know what makes you so dumb, but it works.

MORE STRANGE DEFINITIONS

Cadillac - lack of cattle

Doughnut - holey food

Feather Head - American Indian

First Lady - Eve

Gossip - 24-hour teller

Handicap - a head cover that's easy to find and wear.

Hay - Grass ala mowed

Ideal person - a card player who always wants to deal.

Layaway plan - a burial plan

Overloaded - an elephant riding a bike.

Period - a comma that curled up and went to sleep.

Polygon - the parrot that got away

Primate - removing your spouse from the tv.

Rock music - sung in a rocking chair

Roman - a person who can't settle down.

Scorekeeper - someone who knows the score but keeps it to himself.

Tireless - have a car but no tires

Whether - unpredictable weather

Witchcraft - handmade crafts made for Halloween

She's the first in her family born without a tail.

The story of life is quicker than the wink of an eye; the story of love is hello and goodbye, 'til we meet again.

-Jimi Hendrix

There are only two things I dislike about her–her faces.

I'm glad to see that you're not letting your education get in the way of your ignorance.

I don't want to make a monkey out of you. Why should I take all the credit for something you've done own?

I had a girlfriend who was bi-illiterate. She couldn't read in two languages.

If at first you don't succeed, try again. Then quit. No use being a fool about it.

I have a large seashell collection, which I keep scattered on beaches all over the world.

I must be getting older. Half the stuff in my shopping cart says, "for fast relief."

Hear about the terrorist who hijacked a plane full of lawyers? He threatened to release one every hour if his demands were not met.

I'd give my right arm to be ambidextrous.

In Cleveland, it's illegal to catch mice without a hunting license.

Left Bank - what the robber did when his bag was full of loot.

Money doesn't talk; it goes without saying.

An unemployed court jester is nobody's fool.

Marriage is a mistake every man should make.

You know, it's a long world.
-Lawrence Welk

Man cannot live by bread alone ... unless he's locked in a cage and that's all you're giving him to eat.

A couple of hydrogen atoms walk into a bar. The first says, "I think I lost an electron." "Are you sure?" asks the second. "Yes, I'm positive."

An arctic seal walks into a bar. "What can I get you?" asks the bartender. "Anything but a Canadian Club."

A goldfish flops into a bar. "What can I get you?" asks the bartender. "Water!"

Three men walk into a bar. The 4th one ducks.

An amnesiac walks into a bar and says, "Do I come here often?"

There is always a solution to every problem— neat, plausible and wrong.

H.L.Mencken

Judge: a law student who marks his own papers.

That's a nice suit. Who shines it for you?

All the world's a stage and most of us are desperately unrehearsed.
-Sean O'Casey

An autobiography is the story of how a man thinks he lived.

After one look at this planet any visitor from outer space would say "I WANT TO SEE THE MANAGER."
-William S. Burroughs

Our life is spent trying to find something to do with the time we have rushed through life
trying to save.
-Will Rogers

Life is wasted on the living.

Wife: a former sweetheart.

Legend: a lie that has the dignity of age.

Let us live so that when we die, even the undertaker will be sorry.

-Mark Twain

Life would be so wonderful, if only we knew what to do with it.

-Greta Garbo

Everything I did in my life that was worthwhile, I caught hell for.

-Earl Warren

The trouble with a rat race is that, even if you win, you're still a rat.

-Lily Tomlin

There are good days and there are bad days, and this is one of them.

Historian: an unsuccessful novelist.

When we remember we are all mad, the mysteries disappear and life stands explained.

-Mark Twain

There are only two tragedies. One is not getting what you want and the other is getting it.
-Oscar Wilde

There must be more to life than having it all.

Life is like an onion; you peel off one layer at a time and sometimes you weep.
-Carl Sandburg

Life is just a phase you're going through ... you'll get over it.

Life is divided into the horrible and the miserable.
-Woody Allen

Life is like a cobweb, not an organizational chart.
-Ross Perot.

One way to live longer is to cut out the things you want to live longer for.

If stupidity was music, you'd be a band.

FROM THE LIPS OF YOGI BERRA

Baseball is 90% mental, the other half is physical.

Ninety percent of all mental errors are in your head.

We made too many wrong mistakes.

Nobody goes there nowadays; it's too crowded.

I didn't really say everything I said.

Half the lies they tell about me aren't true.

The future ain't what it used to be.

You over there, pair up in groups of three.

You wouldn't have won, if we'd beat you.

When you come to a fork in the road, take it.

THE WIT OF H.L. MENCKEN

A cynic is a man who, when he smells flowers, looks around for a funeral.

Alimony: the ransom the happy pay to the devil.

All men are frauds. The only difference between them is that some admit it. I myself deny it.

Adultery is the application of democracy to love.

A good politician is quite as unthinkable as an honest burglar.

A man always remembers his first love with special tenderness, but after that he begins to bunch them.

A man may be a fool and not know it, but not if he is married.

Conscience is a mother-in-law whose visit never ends.

Bachelors know more about women than married men; if they didn't, they'd be married too.

An idealist is one who, on noticing that roses smell better than cabbage, concludes that they will also make better soup.

He marries best who puts it off until it's too late.

I detest converts almost as much as I detest missionaries.

Imagine the Creator as a low comedian, and at once the world becomes explicable.

In the United States, doing good has come to be, like patriotism, a favorite device of persons with something to sell.

It is the dull man who is always sure, and the sure man who is always dull.

Reality is only an illusion that occurs due to a lack of alcohol.

Caterpallor: the color you turn after finding half a worm in the fruit you're eating.

Hypochondria is the only disease I haven't got.

Lawyer's creed: a man is innocent until proven broke.

A man walked into a lawyer's office and said, "What are your rates?"
"50 dollars for three questions."
"Isn't that rather steep?"
"Yes," said the lawyer. "And what was your third question?"

An apple a day keeps the doctor away ... and so does having no medical insurance.

As they say at the Planned Parenthood Center, better late than never.

I can see your point, but I still think you're full of crap.

I may be driving slowly, but I'm ahead of you.

Don't bother me. I'm living happily ever after.

I'm not crazy. I've just been in a very bad mood for thirty years.

Where there's smoke, there she is—cooking!

I was thinking of becoming a doctor. I have the handwriting for it.

98% of the time I'm right. Why worry about the other 3%?

There are two kinds of secrets: one is not worth keeping and the other is too good to keep.

There's one good thing about being poor—it's inexpensive.

"I heard you missed school yesterday."
"Not a bit."

Beelzebug: Satan in the form of a mosquito that buzzes in your ear and cannot be cast out.

"How's your wife doing with her diet?"

"Fine. Last night, she vanished."

Memory is what tells a man his wedding anniversary was yesterday.

I asked my wife where she wanted to go for our anniversary. "Some place I've never been," she said. "How about the kitchen, then?"

My wife loves to shop at Bloomingdale's. I bring her mail there twice a week.

All my wife does is shop. Once she was sick for a week and three shops went under.

Living on Earth may be expensive but it includes a annual free trip around the sun.

The blonde drove the wrong way down a one-way street and a cop pulled her over. "Where do you think you're going?" he said. "I must be late," she said. "Everyone is all coming back!"

Here I am! What are your other 2 wishes?

To err is human, to forgive, against company policy.

Life is a moderately good play with a badly-written third act.
-Truman Capote

Life doesn't imitate art; it imitates bad tv.
-Woody Allen

Life is like eating artichokes. You have to go through so much to get so little.

The cost of livin's going up and the chance of livin's going down.
-Flip Wilson

There's nothing that makes you so aware of the improvisation of human existence as a song unfinished. Or an old address book.
-Carson McCullers

FREE PUPPIES. Part Collie, part dog.

I see the mess-up fairy has visited us again.

Q: What happens to a boy during puberty?

A: He leaves his childhood and enters adultery.

If you haven't struck oil in the first three minutes-–stop boring!
-George Jessel

You worry too much about your job. Stop it. You're not paid enough to worry.

When you're swimming in the creek, and an eel bites your cheek ... that's a moray!

How many letters in the alphabet? 19, because ET went home on a UFO and the FBE went after him.

Home is where you hang your @.

Birthdays are good for you. The more you have, the longer you live.

Wear a watch and you'll always know what time it is. Wear two, and you'll never be sure.

Why is sleeping with a man like a soap opera? Just when it's getting interesting, they're finished until next time.

Why do black widow spiders kill their mates? To stop the snoring before it starts.

The hypothalmus is the part of the brain that controls the 4 Fs: fighting, fleeing, feeding --
and mating.
   -anonymous Psychology professor

If you pay peanuts, you get monkeys.

Never judge a book by its movie.

I am free of prejudice. I hate all people equally.
   -W.C. Fields

Aim for the stars. But first aim for their bodyguards.

User: the word computer professionals use when they mean "idiot."

I don't pray because I don't want to bore God.
-Orson Welles

Isn't it strange? The same people who laugh at gypsy fortune tellers take economists seriously.

Procrastination is the greatest labor-saving device of all time.

An apple a day keeps the doctor away, but an onion a day keeps everyone away.

The trouble with being poor is that it takes up all of your time.
-Willem de Kooning

A synonym is a word you use when you can't spell the other one.

The less we know, the longer the explanation.

An economist is an expert who will know tomorrow why the things he predicted yesterday didn't happen today.

A deaf husband and a blind wife are always a happy couple.

Whenever you set out to do something, something else always has to be done first.

-Murphy's Law

A word to the wise ain't necessary; it's the stupid ones that need the advice.

-Bill Cosby

If the sky is the limit, then what is space? Over the limit?

He who laughs, lasts.

The harder you fall, the higher you bounce.

You can never tell which way the train went by looking at the track.

The next time you want to complain, remember: Your garbage disposal probably eats better than 30% of the people in the world.

I hate sex in the movies. Tried it once. The seat folded up, the drink spilled and that ice–well, it really chilled her mood.

Pet Store Sign: Buy one dog, get one flea.

Money can't buy happiness but it sure makes misery easier to live with.

Inside some of us is a thin person struggling to get out, but that person can usually be sedated with a few pieces of chocolate cake.

Where does virgin wool comes from? Ugly sheep.

The Dairy Farmers' Hymn: "What a Friend We Have in Cheeses."

Any man who afflicts the human race with ideas must be prepared to see them misunderstood.
   -H.L. Mencken

I have a drinking problem: no money!

It's hard to make a comeback when you haven't been anywhere.

Democracy is the art and science of running the circus from the monkey cage.

-H.L. Mencken

A carton of yogurt walks into a bar. "We don't serve your kind here," the barman says. "Why not?" says the carton. "I'm cultured!"

Speak when you're angry and you'll make the best speech you'll ever regret.

Alcohol and calculus don't mix. Never drink and derive.

Every girl should use what Mother Nature gave her before Father Time takes it away.

To err is human. To blame it on the computer, even more so.

The cynics are right nine times out of ten.

Eat drink, and be merry, for tomorrow they may make it illegal.

I went alone on my honeymoon. My wife had already seen Niagara Falls.

What is done now is influenced by what you did then, and will determine what you do when now becomes then.

He is not afraid of work; you can tell by the way he fights it.

I'm Canadian. It's like being American, but without the gun.

I was once walking through a forest alone. A tree fell right in front of me. I didn't hear it.

-Stephen Wright

A truly happy person is one who can enjoy the scenery on a detour.

Why are there 5 syllables in "monosyllabic?"

WISDOM OF THE JEWISH MOTHER

Always whisper the name of a disease.

If it tastes good, it's probably not kosher.

Without Jewish mothers, how would psychiatrists make a living?

Without Jewish mothers, how would comedians make a living?

Before you read the menu, look at the prices. If you have to ask the price, you can't afford it. But if you can afford it, tell everyone what you paid.

The important Jewish holidays are the ones where alternate parking is suspended.

Laugh now, but one day you'll be driving a Lexus and eating dinner at four in the afternoon.

Spring ahead, fall back, winter in Boca.

A shmata is a dress your husband's ex has on.

Great One-Liners

According to Jewish dietary law, pork and shellfish may be eaten only in Chinese restaurants

Anything worth saying is worth repeating a thousand times.

After the destruction of the Second Temple, God created Loehmann's.

Where there's smoke, there may be salmon.

No meal is complete without leftovers.

Next year in Jerusalem. The year after that, how about a nice cruise?

WASPs leave and never say goodbye. Jews say goodbye and never leave.

What kind of coat can be put on only when wet? A coat of paint.

The email of the species is more deadly than the mail.

Who was the first person to say, "See that chicken there? I'm gonna eat the first thing that comes out of its butt."

If quizzes are quizzical, what are tests?

Do you know the punishment for bigamy? Two mothers-in-law.

Guy #1: My wife's an angel.

Guy #2: You're lucky. Mine's still alive.

LAWYER: Are you sexually active?

WITNESS: No, I just lie there.

LAWYER: What is your date of birth?

WITNESS: July 9th.

LAWYER: What year?

WITNESS: Every year.

LAWYER: Were you present when your picture was taken?

WITNESS: Would you repeat the question?

OCCUPATIONS

Accountant: someone who knows the cost of everything and the value of nothing.

Auditor: someone who arrives after the battle and bayonets all the wounded.

Statistician: someone who is good with numbers, but lacks the personality to be an accountant.

Actuary: someone who brings a fake bomb on a plane, because that decreases the chances that there will be another, real, bomb on the plane.

Programmer: someone who solves a problem you didn't know you had in a way you don't understand.

Topologist: a person who knows the difference between a coffee cup and a doughnut, but not how to use them.

Lawyer: a person who writes a 10,000-word document and calls it a brief.

Professor: a person who talks in someone else's sleep.

Psychologist: a person who watches everyone else when a beautiful girl walks into the room.

Consultant: a person who takes your watch and tells you the time.

Liberals feel unworthy of their possessions. Conservatives feel they deserve everything they've stolen.

-Mort Sahl

Hockey is a sport for white men. Basketball is a sport for black men. Golf is a sport for white men dressed like black pimps.

-Tiger Woods

If horrific means to make horrible, does terrific mean to make terrible?

LAWYER: All your responses must be oral. Very well, then, what school did you go to?
WITNESS: Oral.

LAWYER: Do you recall the time you examined the body?
WITNESS: The autopsy started at 8:30 P.M.
LAWYER: And he was dead at the time?
WITNESS: No, he was sitting on the table, wondering why I was doing an autopsy.

Testicle: a humorous question in an exam.

LAWYER: Doctor, before you performed the autopsy, did you check for a pulse?
WITNESS: No.
LAWYER: Did you check for blood pressure?
WITNESS: No.
LAWYER: For breathing?
WITNESS: No.
LAWYER: Is it then possible that the patient was alive when you started the autopsy?
WITNESS: No.
LAWYER: How can you be so sure, doctor?
WITNESS: Because his brain was sitting in a jar on my desk.
LAWYER: But could the patient still have been alive nevertheless?
WITNESS: Yes, it is possible that he could have been alive and practicing law.

Every man is thoroughly happy twice in his life: just after he has met his first love and just after he has left his last one.
-H.L. Mencken

My dog can lick anyone!

Televangelists: pro wrestlers of religion.

No matter how bad things get, you got to go on living, even if it kills you.
Sholem Aleichem

Oh, you hate your job? Why didn't you say so? There's a support group for that. It's called EVERYBODY and they meet at the bar.

If you have a lot of tension and you get a headache, do as it says on the aspirin bottle: "Take two aspirin" and "Keep away from children."

If life were fair, Elvis would be alive and all the impersonators would be dead.
-Johnny Carson

The problem with some people is that when they aren't drunk, they're sober.
-William Butler Yeats

Life is a waste of time, time is a waste of life; so get wasted all of the time and have the time of your life.

Constipated people don't give a crap!

When we drink, we get drunk. When we get drunk, we fall asleep. When we fall asleep, we commit no sin. When we commit no sin, we go to heaven. Sooooo let's all get drunk and go to heaven.

-Brian O'Rourke

You can't be a real country unless you have a beer and an airline. It helps if you have some kind of a football team, or some nuclear weapons. But at the very least you need a beer.

-Frank Zappa

Always remember that I have taken more out of alcohol than alcohol has taken out of me.

-Winston Churchill

A hole has been found in the nudist colony wall. The police are looking into it.

He who survives mustard gas and pepper spray is a seasoned veteran.

Did you hear about the new Divorce Barbie? It comes with all of Ken's stuff.

REAL ACTUAL SIGNS

Toilet out of order. Please use floor below.

Automatic washing machines: please remove all your clothes when the light goes out.

Bargain basement upstairs.

Would the person who took the stepladder yesterday please return it or further steps will be taken.

The farmer allows walkers to cross the field free. But the bull charges.

After coffee break, staff should empty the pot and stand upside down on the drainboard.

We can repair anything. (Please knock hard on the door - the bell doesn't work.)

For anyone who has children and doesn't know it, there is a day care on the first floor.

If you cannot read, this leaflet will tell you how to get lessons.

Warning: the consumption of alcohol may create the illusion that you are tougher, smarter, faster and better looking than most people.

Plagarism saves time.

Warning: the consumption of alcohol may cause pregnancy.

They say, "If you can't beat them, join them." Well, I say, "If you can't beat them, beat them" because they'll be expecting you to join them and you'll have the element of surprise.

My opinions may have changed, but not the fact that I am right.

The Vote is the instrument and symbol of a free person's power to make a fool of himself, and a wreck of his country.
    -Ambrose Bierce

What right does Congress have to go around making laws just because they deem it necessary?
    -Marion Barry, mayor of Washington, D.C.

If ignorance goes to $40 a barrel, I want drilling rights to George Bush's head.
    -Jim Hightower

A lawyer's great when a felon needs a friend.

Politics is the art of looking for trouble, finding it everywhere, diagnosing it incorrectly, and applying the wrong remedies.

-Groucho Marx

I discovered that I scream the same way whether I'm about to be devoured by a great white shark or if a piece of seaweed touches my foot.

A $200 picture tube will protect a 10-cent fuse by blowing first.

Science is true. Don't be misled by fact.

Simple jobs will always be put off, because there will be time to do them later.

Cream rises to the top, but so does scum.

No matter what goes wrong, there's always someone who knew it would.

Things equal to nothing else are equal to each other.

When putting something into memory, remember where you put it.

When somebody drops something, everyone will kick it around instead of picking it up.

If at first you don't succeed, try management.

If you can't fix it with a hammer, you've got an electrical problem.

Computer dating is fine–if you're a computer.
-Rita Mae Brown

Computers are like Old Testament gods; lots of rules and no mercy.
-Joseph Campbell

Computers are useless. They can only give you answers.
-Pablo Picasso

If you don't know how to do something, you don't know how to do it with a computer, either.

Anyone who has lost track of time when using a computer knows the propensity to dream, the urge to make dreams come true and the tendency to miss lunch.
-Tim Berners-Lee

Although golf was originally restricted to wealthy, overweight Protestants, today it's open to anybody who owns hideous clothing.
-Dave Barry

Golf is more fun than walking naked in a strange place, but not much.
-Buddy Hackett

Give me golf clubs, fresh air and a beautiful partner, and you can keep the clubs and the fresh air.
-Jack Benny

Big business never pays a nickel in taxes, according to Ralph Nader, who represents a big consumer organization that never pays a nickel in taxes.
-Dave Barry

The greatest remedy for anger is delay.

Business? It's quite simple. Other peoples'
money.

Catch a man a fish, and you can sell it to him.
Teach a man to fish, and you ruin a wonderful
business opportunity.

Don't gamble. Take all your savings and buy
some good stock and hold it until it goes up, then sell
it. If it don't go up, don't buy it.
    -Will Rogers

Employees make the best dates. You don't have
to pick them up and they're always tax-deductible.
    -Andy Warhol

By faithfully working 8 hours a day, you may
eventually get to be boss and work 12 hours a day.
    -Robert Frost

I always said that mega-mergers were for
magalomaniacs.
    -David Ogilvy

Beware the fury of the patient man.

He who lives by the crystal ball soon learns to eat ground glass.

When angry, count four. When very very angry, swear.
> -Mark Twain

I hate graffiti. In fact, I hate all Italian food.

An honest politician is one who, when he is bought, will stay bought.

A politician is a fellow who will lay down your life for his country.

If you want a friend in Washington, get a dog.
> -Harry S. Truman

Some guys get credit for being conservative when they're only stupid.

Robbers demand your money or your life; women require both.

Being a woman is a terribly difficult task, since it consists chiefly in dealing with men.

Americans like fat books and skinny women.
-Russell Baker

A woman without a man is like a fish without a bicycle.
-Gloria Steinem

Being a woman is of special interest only to aspiring male transsexuals. To actual women, it is simply a good excuse not to play football.
-Fran Lebowitz

Don't give a woman advice; one should never give a woman anything she can't wear in the evening.
-Oscar Wilde

Age to women is like Kryptonite to Superman.

Bozone: The substance surrounding stupid people that stops bright ideas from penetrating. The bozone layer, unfortunately, shows little signs of breaking down in the near future.

An acquaintance is a person whom we know well enough to borrow from, but not well enough to lend to.

A nation is not in danger of financial disaster simply because it owes itself money.

Don't stay in bed unless you can make money in bed.
    -George Burns

I don't mind going back to daylight saving time. With inflation, the hour will be the only thing I've saved all year.
    -Victor Borge

I don't like money, actually, but it quiets my nerves.
    -Joe Louis

Don't marry for money. You can borrow it cheaper.

If you see a bandwagon, it's too late.

I love to visit Washington, if only to be nearer to my money.
   -Bob Hope

It's amazing how fast later comes, when you buy now!
   -Milton Berle

Money can't buy friends, but you can get a better class of enemies.

Never invest in anything that eats or needs repairing.

Money can't buy happiness; it can, however, rent it.

The meek shall inherit the earth, but not the mineral rights.
   -J. Paul Getty

When a fellow says, "It ain't the money, it's the principle of the thing," it's the money.

When one barber shaves another, who talks?

We used to build civilizations. Now we build shopping malls.

People will buy anything that's "one to a customer."

The other line always moves faster.

You never realize how short a month is until you pay alimony.

A great fortune is a great slavery.

Behind every great fortune is a great crime.

It is better to spend money like there's no tomorrow than to spend tonight like there's no money.

Pro football is like nuclear warfare. There are no winners, only survivors.

Race drivers have one foot on the brake, one on the clutch, and one on the throttle.

-Bob Varsha

The other teams could make trouble for us if they win.

-Yogi Berra

Sports is the toy department of human life.

Rugby is a beastly game played by gentlemen; soccer is a gentleman's game played by beasts. Football is a beastly game played by beasts.

The most popular labor-saving device is still money

Someday I want to be rich. Some people get so rich they lose all respect for humanity. That's how rich I want to be.

-Rita Rudner

Too many people spend money they haven't earned, to buy things they don't want, to impress people they don't like.

There's no reason to be the richest man in the cemetery. You can't do business from there.

A psychiatrist is a fellow who asks you expensive questions your wife asks for nothing.

A doctor lost his practice. Desperate, he tried to hold up a bank, but they couldn't read his writing.

The difference between an itch and an allergy is about fifty dollars.

I don't mind being a grandfather except that it means I'm sleeping with a grandmother.

Nowadays, when a commencement speaker tells the graduates that the future is theirs... is that a promise or a threat?

Considering the alternative, life isn't such a bad deal after all.

I wouldn't believe him if he swore he was lying.

The cooing stops after the honeymoon; the billing goes on forever.

I was surrounded by a lion and a bull. I shot the lion first because I could always shoot the bull.

The baby, a girl, was born two days later than expected. Holding her, her father said, "Only two minutes old and already you've kept a man waiting."

Amnesia is nature's way of saying "Forget it!"

Asking an incumbent member of Congress to vote for term limits is like asking a chicken to vote for Colonel Sanders.

A politician is a person with whose ideas you don't agree; if you think he's right, he's a statesman.

Giving money and power to a government is like giving whisky and the car keys to a teenaged boy.

I will make a bargain with the Republicans. If they will stop telling lies about Democrats, we will stop telling the truth about them.
     -Adlai Stevenson

You're stressed when you can hear mimes.

He who steals my purse steals trash. What a dumb place to put trash!

Behind every successful man is a surprised woman.

If you want something, ask a man; if you want something done, ask a woman.
    -Margaret Thatcher

If you want to know the value of money, try to borrow some.

To err is human. To admit it isn't.

I installed my DVR myself. Now I get movies on my electric can opener.

I asked my secretary to take a letter. She picked N.

First I was bullish, then I was bearish, and now I'm just brokish!

It's good to live in a city where millions of people who live close to one another spend their time being lonely.

I'm not saying my wife doesn't know how to cook but we have a complete set of soup knives.

Good girls go to heaven; bad girls go everywhere.

Guys are like dogs. They keep coming back. Girls are like cats. Yell at a cat once ... it's gone!
    -Lenny Bruce

I'd much rather be a woman than a man. Women can cry, they can wear cute clothes, and they're the first to be rescued off a sinking ship.
    -Gilda Radner

Money is better than poverty, if only for financial reasons.
    -Woody Allen

Of course I don't look busy. I got it right the first time.

It's hard to tell what really brings happiness. Both poverty and wealth have failed.

Whatever women do, they must do twice as well as men to be thought half as good. Luckily, this is not difficult.

Women now have choices. They can be married, not married, have a job, not have a job, be married with children, unmarried with children. Men have the same choices they've always had: work or prison.

Women ... can't live with 'em ... can't shoot 'em.
-Ivan Turgenev

I'm not a member of any organized political party. I'm a Democrat.
-Will Rogers

If I were two-faced, would I be wearing this one?
-Abraham Lincoln

Nothing lasts forever—except a bad play.

Great One-Liners

My choice early in life was either to be a piano player in a whorehouse or a politician. And to tell the truth, there's hardly any difference.
-Harry S. Truman

A statesman is a dead politician.

The other day on the golf course, I broke 70. That's a lot of golf clubs.
-Henny Youngman

I think it's wrong that only one company makes the game MONOPOLY.
-Stephen Wright

It's easy to make a buck. It's a lot tougher to make a difference.
-Tom Brokaw

There was a time when a fool and his money were soon parted but now it happens to everyone.

There's no business like show business but there are several businesses like accounting.
-David Letterman

Home computers are being called upon to perform many new functions, including the consumption of homework formerly eaten by the dog.

This is what's cool about working with computers: they don't argue, they remember everything, and they don't drink all your beer.

The marriage of Joe DiMaggio and Marilyn Monroe? I don't know if it's good for baseball, but it sure beats the hell out of rooming with Phil Rizzuto!
   -Yogi Berra

Too much love is not even enough.

Getting married is very much like going to a restaurant with friends. You order what you want, then when you see what the other fellow has, you wish you had ordered that.

I used to sell furniture. The trouble was, it was my own.

Mine was a voice crying in the wilderness. The next time I take a road trip, I'll bring a map.

All my wife wanted on Valentine's Day was a little card - preferably American Express.

It's getting so there's no money in money.

I vacationed in a place with sea, sand, and surf. I came back bushed, burned, and busted.

The best vacation ever: buy a new van, put the kids in the back, and take a cruise.

Don't let your mind wander. It's too small to be let out alone.

If you woke up breathing, congratulations. You have another chance.

I made a killing on Wall Street today. I shot my broker!

And now a word from Wall Street—HELP!

On Wall Street you have bears, bulls, and—if you count my stocks—dogs.

Great One-Liners

The best things in life are free ... or at least have no interest or payments for one full year.

He's really tough. He went to reform school on a scholarship.

"Hey, Mom, is that dinner I smell?"
"It is, and you do."

After four karate lessons, I can now break a two-inch board with my cast.

Experience teaches only the teachable.

Two kids were playing doctor. One of them said, "You operate and I'll sue."

To those of you graduating today who received honors, awards and distinctions, I say well done. And to the "C" students, I say you too may one day be president of the United States.
-George W. Bush

Fans, don't fail to miss tomorrow's game.
-Dizzy Dean

I believe in rules, sure I do. If there weren't any rules, how could you break them?
-Leo Durocher

The key to being a good manager is keeping the people who hate me away from those who are still undecided.
-Casey Stengel

Golf: a costly way to play marbles.

The kid doesn't chew tobacco, smoke, drink, curse, or chase broads. I don't see how he can possibly make it.
-Richie Ashburn

You don't realize how easy this game is until you get up in that broadcasting booth.
-Mickey Mantle

The Expos' fans discovered that "boo" is pronounced the same in French as in English.
-Harry Caray

To err is human. To shrug is Civil Service.

ITEMS OF INTEREST FROM SYNAGOGUE NOTICES

Don't let worry kill you. Let your synagogue help. Join us after service. Remember in prayer the many who are sick of our congregation.

There will be a meeting of the Little Mothers Club. All women wishing to become Little Mothers please see the rabbi in his private study.

The Men's Club is warmly invited to the party hosted by the Women's Club. Refreshments will be served for a nominal feel.

Weight Watchers will meet at 7 PM at the Community Center. Please use the large double door at the side entrance.

A bean supper will be held Monday evening in the community center. Music will follow.

Rabbi is on vacation. Massages can be given to his secretary.

If you enjoy sinning, the choir is looking for you.

The Associate Rabbi unveiled the synagogue's new fundraising campaign slogan this week: "I Upped My Pledge. Now Up Yours."

The ladies of Hadassah have cast off clothing of every kind and they may be seen in the basement every Tuesday.

Basically, my wife was immature. I'd be in the bath and she'd come in and sink my boats.
-Woody Allen

Football incorporates the two worst elements of American society: violence, punctuated by committee meetings.
-George Will

Education is what you get when you read the fine print. Experience is what you get if you don't.
-Aldous Huxley

Always write angry letters to your enemies. Never mail them.

I'm living so far beyond my income that we may almost be said to be living apart.
-e.e.cummings

I got rid of my husband. The cat was allergic.

Bridge is a game that separates the men from the boys. It also separates husbands and wives.

I married the first man I ever kissed. When I tell this to my children, they just about throw up.
  -Barbara Bush

Every time I start thinking too much about how I look, I just find a Happy Hour and by the time I leave, I look just fine.

Palestinian little girl to her mother: "After Abdul blows himself up, can I have his room?"

A government which robs Peter to pay Paul can always depend on the support of Paul.
  -George Bernard Shaw

I don't make jokes. I just watch the government and report the facts.
  -Will Rogers

If you think health care is expensive now, wait until you see what it costs when it's free!
  -P.J. O'Rourke

I jog everywhere for my health but I never find it.

A little girl was diligently pounding away on her grandfather's computer keyboard. She told him she was writing a story. "What's it about?" he asked. "I don't know," she replied. "I can't read."

Are Eskimos God's frozen people?

It's easy to see why they drink tea in the UK. Just try their coffee!

A woman says to the judge: "That's my side of the story. Now let me tell you his."

There's only one problem with buying on time. When you get sick of something, you finally own it.

Sign seen on a store: If you're interested in finding out whether there's life after death, try robbing this store.

Nothing's more expensive than a girl who's free for the evening.

My wife won't give me a divorce until she can find a way of doing it without making me happy.

AN ODE TO ENGLISH LANGUAGE PLURALS

We'll begin with a box and the plural is boxes.

But the plural of ox becomes oxen, not oxes.

One fowl is a good, but two are called geese.

Yet the plural of moose should never be meese.

You may call a lone mouse or a nest full of mice.

Yet the plural of house is houses, not hice.

If the plural of man is always called men

Why shouldn't the plural of pan be called pen?

If I speak of my foot and show you my feet

And I give you a boot, would a pair be called beet?

If one is a tooth and a whole set are teeth

Why shouldn't the plural of booth be called beeth?

And one may be that and three would be those

Yet hat in the plural would never be hose

And the plural of cat is cats and not cose.

We speak of a brother and also of brethren

But though we say mother, we never say methren.

Then the masculine pronouns are he, his and him

But imagine the feminine: she, shis and shim!

And in closing, if Father is Pop

How come then that Mother's not Mop?

My dog had worms and the vet told me to feed him garlic. Now his bark is <u>really</u> worse than his bite.

In the UK, a guy who doesn't do anything is called a gentleman. Here, we call him a bum.

I found Jesus. He was hiding in my trunk when I got back from Tijuana.

Sign in a barbershop window: SIX BARBERS. CONTINUOUS DISCUSSION.

I know a bar that has a little person as a bartender, to make the drinks look bigger.

That baseball team has been in the cellar so long, it's damp.

"Help me. I haven't eaten in three days."
"Force yourself."

Rain is strange: it makes flowers come up and taxis disappear.

QUESTIONS THAT STUMPED DEAR ABBY

Dear Abby: What can I do about all the sex, nudity, language and violence on my VCR?

Dear Abby: I have a man I never could trust. He cheats so much. I'm not even sure this baby I'm carrying is his!

Dear Abby: Our son is taking Judo. Why would a boy who was raised in a good Christian home turn against his own?

Dear Abby: You told some woman whose husband had lost all interest in sex to send him to a doctor. Well, my husband lost all interest in sex years ago, and he _is_ a doctor.

Dear Abby: I suspected that my husband had been fooling around, and when I confronted him with the evidence, he denied everything and said it would never happen again.

Dear Abby: My mother's mean and short tempered. Is she going through her mental pause?

Great One-Liners

A man walks over to a New York City taxi and asks the driver, "Can you tell me where the Guggenheim Museum is, or should I go screw myself?"

My wife is a religious cook. Everything she makes is a burnt offering.

Many a good hanging prevents a bad marriage.
-Wm. Shakespeare

Men think monogamy is something you make dining tables out of.

Mom and Pop were just a couple of kids when they got married. He was 18, she was 16, I was 3.
-Billie Holliday

Keep your eyes wide open before marriage, and half shut afterwards.

The way to get things done is not to mind who gets the credit for doing them.

When in doubt, mumble; when in trouble, delegate; when in charge, ponder.

GREAT QUOTES ABOUT MARRIAGE

I'd never be unfaithful to my wife, because I love my house very much.

In life, it's not who you know that's important, it's how your wife found out.
-Joey Adams

I've never been married, but I tell people I'm divorced so they won't think there's something wrong with me.
-Elayne Boosler

If love means never having to say you're sorry, then marriage means always having to say everything twice.
-Estelle Getty

I never mind my wife having the last word. In fact, I'm delighted when she gets to it.
-Walter Matthau

Marriage is nature's way of keeping us from fighting with strangers.
-Alan King

I never married because there was no need. I have 3 pets at home which answer the same purpose as a husband. I have a dog which growls every morning, a parrot which swears all afternoon, and a cat that comes home late at night.
    -Marie Corelli

Many a good hanging prevents a bad marriage.
-Wm. Shakespeare

Marriage is like a bank account. You put it in, you take it out, you lose interest.
    -Irwin Corey

My husband said it was him or the cat ... gee, I miss him sometimes.

My husband said he needed more space. So I locked him outside.
    -Roseanne Barr

Lust is the sin that gets me excited. Luckily, I'm married, so I get really good jewelry out of it.
    -Heather Locklear

Never trust a husband too far or a bachelor too near.
-Helen Rowland

Real happiness is when you marry a girl for love and then find out she has money.
-Bob Monkhouse

Once you are married, there is nothing for you, not even suicide, but to be good.
-Robert Louis Stevenson

My wife Mary and I have been married for 47 years, and not once have we had an argument serious enough for divorce; murder, yes, but divorce, never.
-Jack Benny

The best way to get most husbands to do something is to suggest that perhaps they're too old to do it.
-Anne Bancroft

One's fantasy goes for a walk and returns with a bride.
-Bernard Malamud

The only time some fellows are seen with their wives is after they're indicted.
-Kin Hubbard

There were three of us in this marriage, so it was a bit crowded.
-Diana, Princess of Wales

Your marriage is in trouble if your wife says, "You're only interested in one thing," and you can't remember what it is.
-Milton Berle

You have no idea of the women I <u>didn't</u> marry.
-Artie Shaw

There was an old man of Lyme who married 3 wives at a time. When asked, "Why a third?" he replied: "One's absurd and bigamy, sir, is a crime!"
-William Cosmo Monkhouse

With my wife, I don't get no respect. I made a toast on her birthday to "the best woman a man ever had." The waiter joined me.
-Rodney Dangerfield

If a company can't explain – in one sentence - what it does ... it's illegal.
-Lewis Black

Sign in a bar: If you're drinking to forget, please pay in advance.

My definition of a redundancy is an air bag in a politician's car.
-Larry Hagman

On one side you have book burners, Congressional wives and Pat Robertson. On the other side, you have vulgar comedians, foul-mouthed rap groups and Dennis Hopper. All your choices in life should be so easy!
-Sandra Bernhard

One of my movies was called "True Lies." It's what the Democrats should have called their Convention.
-Arnold Schwarzenegger

Now and then an innocent man is sent to the Legislature.
-Kin Hubbard

Latinos for Republicans. It's like roaches for Raid.

-John Leguizamo

It is fast approaching the point where I don't want to elect anyone stupid enough to want the job of President.

-Erma Bombeck

There's no trick to being a humorist when you have the whole government working for you.

-Will Rogers

There is one sure way of telling when politicians aren't telling the truth ... their lips move.

-Felicity Kendall

Today, the L.A. Times accused Arnold Schwarzenegger of groping six women. I'm telling you, this guy is presidential material.

-David Letterman

We're half the people; we should be half the Congress.

-Jeanndette Rankin

You can lead a man to Congress, but you can't make him think.
-Milton Berle

When women kiss, it always reminds me of prizefighters shaking hands.
-H.L. Mencken

Cosmetics is a boon to every woman, but a girl's best friend is still a nearsighted man.
-Yoko Ono

You can fool some of the people all the time, and those are the ones you want to concentrate on.
-George W. Bush

For me, the worst part of playing golf, by far, has always been hitting the ball.
-Dave Barry

The company I work for is so stressful our computer has an ulcer.

My wife isn't talking to me today and I'm in no mood to interrupt her.

MAN #1: It got married because I was sick and tired of going to the laundromat, eating out, and wearing torn clothes.

MAN #2: I got divorced for the same reasons.

A diamond is forever; the payments are longer.

Two drunks found themselves on a roller coaster. "We're making great time," said one. "But I'm not sure we're on the right bus."

There was a convict who was a disgrace to his uniform.

A Martian returned to his planet and was debriefed: "Is there any life on Earth?"
He replied, "A little, on Saturday night."

I know a very shy guy. His answering machine says: "I'm in right now, but you probably don't want to talk to me."

Golf is a really fascinating game. It's taken me forty years to discover that I can't play it.

THANKS FOR ALL YOUR EDUCATIONAL EMAILS!

I no longer open a public bathroom door without using a paper towel.

I can't use the remote in a hotel room because how do I know what the last person was doing while flipping through the channels.

I have trouble shaking hands with someone who has been driving because the #1 pastime while driving alone is picking one's nose.

I no longer have any savings because I gave it all to a sick girl who is about to die in the hospital for the 1,387,564th time.

I can't touch any woman's purse for fear she may have put it on a public bathroom floor.

I no longer drink Pepsi or Dr. Pepper since the people who make those products are atheists who refuse to put "under God" on their cans.

Because of your concern I no longer drink any cola because it can remove toilet stains.

I no longer drive my car because I now know I can't buy gas from certain companies.

And thanks for letting me know I can't boil water in the microwave because it will blow up in my face.

Send this message to six of your best friends, put your name on the top of the list, and you'll get endless emails in return. Good luck!

A woman can smell mink through twelve inches of lead.
-Groucho Marx

Everywhere you look, there are signs saying, "Washington slept here." No wonder he's called the father of our country!

A woman has seven ages—the real one and six wild guesses.

No woman will ever go to the moon. She wouldn't know what to wear.

The best way to keep looking young is to hang out with old people.

He took his girl to the zoo, but the zoo wouldn't accept her.

They ask, "Death, where is thy sting?" It's in the funeral expenses, dummy!

Our liquor company pays time and a fifth.

She had to go to the Virgin Islands under an assumed name.

Do not argue with an idiot. He will drag you down to his level and beat you with experience.

The probability of someone watching you is proportional to the stupidity of what you're doing.

I don't have an attitude; I have a personality you can't handle.

The best way to lie is to tell the truth – carefully edited truth.

A positive attitude may not solve all your problems; but it will annoy enough people to make it worth the effort.

It matters not whether you win or lose; it matters whether or not I win or lose.

No one is listening until you fart.

What's the most important thing to learn in chemistry? Don't lick the spoon.

Life's like a bird. It's pretty cute until it shits on your head.

Everything is edible. Some things are only edible once.

The knack of flying is learning how to throw yourself at the floor and miss.

Everyone has the right to be stupid, but you are abusing the privilege.

I love to give homemade gifts. Which of my kids would you like?

Failure is not falling down; it's not getting up again.

If you want to be a leader, just drive at the speed limit on a two-lane wandering country road.

The difference between genius and stupidity is that genius has its limits.

"Waiter, what's that fly doing in my soup?"
"Looks like the backstroke to me."

A couple together in bed. MAN: I'm going to make you the happiest woman in the world. WOMAN: I'll miss you.

I love golf. I live golf. I dream golf. If only I could play golf!

MAN: I'm washing my sweatshirt. What setting should I use on the machine?
WOMAN: Depends. What does it say on the shirt?
MAN: Syracuse University.

A golf club walks into a bar. The bartender refuses to serve him, "because you'll be driving."

I can please only one person per day. Today is not your day. Tomorrow isn't looking good either.

Somehow I'm getting stronger as I get older. Last year, I couldn't carry $30-worth of groceries. This year, it's easy.

I'm as sound as a dollar, but I'll get better.

Procrastinate Now!

The trouble with life is there's no background music.

I smile because I don't know what the hell is going on.

It's better to have loved and lost. Much better!

At a Hawaiian luau they eat with their fingers. I have a family at home exactly like that.

I ruined my health by drinking to other peoples'.

Money can't buy happiness. It just helps you look for it in many more places.

PATIENT: I'd like a second opinion.
DOCTOR: All right, I'll tell you again.

"Do you believe in reincarnation?"
"I eat it every day. It's called hash."

Power corrupts. Absolute power is pretty neat, though.

If evolution is outlawed, only outlaws will evolve.

Anyone else notice that "zebra" is an anagram of "dyslexia?"

I've never understood decimals. I can't see the point.

314 backwards spells PIE.

A drunk sees a man looking under the hood of his car. "Wassup?" says the drunk. The man says. "Piston broke." "Yeah," says the drunk. "Me, too."

I wouldn't do volunteer work if they paid me.

REMEMBER THE ORIGINAL HOLLYWOOD SQUARES? Peter Marshall asked the questions and the answers were strictly spontaneous and unscripted.

Q: True or false, a pea can last 5,000 years.
George Gobel: Boy, it sure seems that way sometimes.

Q: You've been having trouble sleeping. Are you probably a man or a woman?
Don Knotts: That's what's been keeping me awake.

Q:Do female frogs croak?
Paul Lynde: If you hold their little heads under the water long enough.

Q: Which of your 5 senses diminishes with age?
Charley Weaver: My sense of decency.

Q: Can boys join the Camp Fire Girls?
Marty Allen: Only after lights out.

Q: In bowling, what's a perfect score?
Rose Marie: Ralph, the pin boy.

Q: Why do Hell's Angels wear leather?
Paul Lynde: Because chiffon wrinkles too easily.

Q: According to Ann Landers, what are two things you should never do in bed?
Paul Lynde: Point and laugh.

Q: Jackie Gleason recently revealed that he firmly believes in them and has actually seen them? What?
Charley Weaver: His feet.

GREAT
ONE
LINERS